AMATEUR BOXING
MENTAL STRESS & STRENGTH

Nathan E. Lavid, MD

Copyrighted Material

Amateur Boxing: Mental Stress & Strength

Copyright © 2018 by NEL Books. All Rights Reserved.

No part of this publication may be reproduced, stored in a retrieval system or transmitted, in any form or by any means—electronic, mechanical, photocopying, recording or otherwise—without prior written permission from the publisher, except for the inclusion of brief quotations in a review.

For information about this title or to order other books and/or electronic media, contact the publisher:
NEL Books
65 Pine Avenue
Long Beach, CA 90802
www.mentalstrengthinboxing.com

Library of Congress Control Number: 2018912040

978-1-7328614-0-4 (Hardcover)
978-1-7328614-1-1 (Softcover)
978-1-7328614-2-8 (eBook)

Printed in the United States of America

Cover and Interior design: Jeff Chabot

Publisher's Cataloging-In-Publication Data

Names: Lavid, Nathan, author.
Title: Amateur boxing : mental stress & strength / Nathan E. Lavid, MD.
Description: Long Beach, CA : NEL Books, [2018] | Includes bibliographical references.
Identifiers: ISBN 9781732861404 (hardcover) | ISBN 9781732861411 (softcover) | ISBN 9781732861428 (ebook)
Subjects: LCSH: Boxing--Psychological aspects. | Boxing--Training. | Stress tolerance (Psychology)
Classification: LCC GV706.4 .L38 2018 (print) | LCC GV706.4 (ebook) | DDC 796.01--dc23

To Benjamin and Samuel

CONTENTS

Acknowledgments — vii
Introduction — ix

Part I: The Mental Stress of Boxing — 1

1. Boxing, The Sport — 5
2. The Neuroscience of Fear — 25
3. The Neuroscience of Anticipatory Anxiety — 41

Part II: Transforming Mental Stress to Strength: Boxing Smart — 49

4. Six Weeks Out: Boxing Skills — 53
5. Three Weeks Out: Boxing Strategy and Ring Craft — 65
6. Two Days Out: You Versus You — 79
7. The Bout: You Versus Him — 95

Part III: Why Box? — 109

8. Mental Benefits — 113
9. Outside the Ring — 119

Epilogue: Randie Carver   **127**
   Bibliography   133
   About the Author   139

ACKNOWLEDGMENTS

I AM INDEBTED TO many for this book. First and foremost, to those who read drafts and shared their constructive thoughts. My aunt, Linda Lavid, an accomplished writer and artist, read my initial draft. With kindness, she offered criticism that was encouraging. Jonathan Starke, a writer and former amateur boxer, gave a sound and appreciated critique to an early draft. My assistant, Thida Yang, brought up smart and interesting suggestions to various excerpts when I was concerned about their relevance and clarity. Aviva Layton, a top-ranked professional in the writing world, provided her needed editorial expertise. Chris Jurewicz, a talented artist and amateur boxer, who is also a former opponent and now friend. Chris was the first person I reached out to when considering writing this book and lent his thoughtful support throughout the project.

The figures needed for this book were inherently difficult. I needed both informative scientific and humanistic figures, pleasing to the eye for all ages. Thankfully, Jeff Chabot provided the art direction and Jason González generated the illustrations that met these requirements and my gratitude.

This book would not have materialized if not for my firsthand experience as an amateur boxer. I owe many thanks to the many coaches, officials, fellow boxers, family, and friends who have guided and supported me through my journeys in the ring. And I would probably not have taken these journeys if not first brought to the boxing gym by my mother. Mom, I could always hear you. This book belongs to you. A"H.

INTRODUCTION

IF YOU HAVE NOT been in a fight, it is coming. You can avoid conflict, take the path of least resistance, and practice nonviolence, but you will still be in a fight one day. You are also going to get punched in the face. This punch will be delivered without warning, and you may not even see it coming. These are the ones that hurt the most. You can scoff, shout me down, and call me a liar. Denial is no escape. Life, inevitability, will bring the fight to you.

This fight may not be physical, but, like all fights, it will be threatening and evoke negative emotions. These emotions are the mental stress of the fight. This mental stress may make the fight harder than it is and may even defeat you before you have begun to fight.

The mental challenges experienced during your fight will be difficult. Nature dictates this, but these challenges are not insurmountable. This negativity can be transformed into positive action and thoughts because you are born with the capacity to fight and meet this challenge. However, how developed this capacity is in all of us varies. Some may have the inherent ability to address danger head on. Some may not. Though, no matter how well you can fight, you will get better with practice.

This is why you should box. You box to practice addressing the mental challenges that you will experience outside the ring. The same emotions evoked by boxing are the same emotions that you will experience outside the ring during your fight. This is one of the benefits of boxing, which is an ancient sport. A sport that has persisted because it exercises the whole person, both the body and brain.

The focus of this book is amateur boxing. Boxing as a profession is for a select few, but amateur boxing is for everyone. Now, with the sanctioning of female and older competitors, the only limitation is a medical condition that prevents participation. From a mental standpoint, amateur boxing is useful and provides value with a time-honed methodology and forum to address stress and transform it into strength. This mental strength emerges from mental stress. There is no other pathway. The training in amateur boxing acknowledges this pathway and provides guidance on how this mental stress can be used to your advantage; how it develops positive mental and physical strength.

Amateur boxing transforms this mental stress to strength and this forum is presented from three vantage points. One is from a scientific standpoint. Being a psychiatrist, a large portion of my professional life is addressing mental processes from a scientific perspective. Two, from my experiences as an amateur boxer. Three, from my experiences shadowing and working as a ringside physician before I exclusively practiced psychiatry.

This is an attempt to aid the novice amateur boxer who has not yet entered competition or has just had a few bouts, as well as to encourage the curious reader to take up the sport. For simplicity, I use masculine pronouns, but they are used in the generic sense.

INTRODUCTION

The material within is applicable to us all. There are no distinctions or specifiers needed for culture, race, or gender.

The science presented is influenced by my psychiatric practice. Clinically, the therapeutic usefulness of scientific knowledge varies in each patient. Some patients request and respond to the intellectual enrichment provided by contemporary psychiatric understanding. These patients benefit from reviews of medical literature and the model of the brain I have in my office. Other patients find the substance of scientific knowledge is better appreciated by the findings. Explanation is not requested or needed. Applying this clinical tool is independent of the age and education of my patients. When first caring for a patient, I never know which approach is best. It is only after we have had time together, to size each other up, that the proper therapeutic approach becomes apparent.

Considering how the usefulness of science will vary for each reader, I have simplified much of it and included anatomical and schematic figures to clarify the material. However, the science of the brain and nervous system, termed "neuroscience," is not a simple topic. While I have simplified much of the neuroscience, I have refrained from oversimplification. Chapters 2 and 3 are devoted to the neuroscience of the mental stress you will experience and delve into the evolutionary and biological basis for your emotions. As the brain is a complex organ, this information is technical and dense. For these two chapters, I provide a list of take-home points at the beginning of each chapter. I recommend reading these take-home points, skipping over the text and reviewing the figures. Then continue reading the book.

When first boxing, you will experience strong emotions before and during your bout. These are also the same emotions that you will experience outside the ring. You may question if this mental stress is normal. It is. Revisit chapters 2 and 3 when you are wondering a bit more why you feel the way that you do. You will have a better appreciation for the material. Also, for those readers who wish to pursue the science in greater detail, I have provided a bibliography that contains the source material.

I am not an Olympic champion or had any boxing proficiency or potential to consider it as an occupation, but I have been involved with amateur boxing since I was a young boy. I have never regretted any of my time expended on boxing and have gained an enormous amount from the sport. It seems fitting, that as a physician, I was introduced to amateur boxing by my pediatrician. By the time I was six years old, I developed the ability to ignore my parents' directions to the extent they thought I might be becoming deaf. The audiologist thought otherwise. My pediatrician, knowing now my hearing was normal, suggested I might have what then was referred to as Attention Deficit Disorder (ADD). He offered a trial of stimulant medication, which my mother declined. Enrolling me in sports where I could learn discipline and expend some energy was then brought up. Soon after, I was enrolled in a boxing program at a YMCA in Buffalo, New York.

I have been in and out of amateur boxing ever since. As a youth, I left amateur boxing and pursued other sports. I revisited boxing in college and medical school. Also, during medical school, I would assist ringside physicians at boxing shows.

After medical school, I stopped competing, but worked as a volunteer ringside physician during my internship and residency when I still practiced general medicine. During my subspecialty training in forensic psychiatry, I left amateur boxing again.

I returned to amateur boxing in my forties, when I started taking my two young boys to a boxing gym close to our home in Long Beach, California. Long Beach United Boxing Club has an amateur program. One of the owners and operators of the Club,

INTRODUCTION

Doug MacKinnon, who was teaching my boys to box, made me aware of Masters Boxing. Masters Boxing is competitive amateur boxing for those over thirty-five. Masters Boxing has all the safety regulations of amateur boxing, with additional precautions of using large gloves heavily padded at sixteen ounces.

Doug, being around the same age as me, asked if I was interested in entering a Masters Boxing show. He had signed up and was offering me an opportunity to box out of his gym with the same trainers and seconds he was using, all of whom were familiar to me from the gym. I was soon back in the ring with a younger heart.

Through my boxing experience, including unsanctioned bouts, I have had twenty amateur bouts, seven of them as a Masters boxer. I have done well, more so as a Masters boxer, winning Championship belts at 178 pounds in the 2016 Ringside National Masters Tournament and the 2017 Southern California State Amateur Boxing Championships. I have also lost. My overall record is ten wins and ten losses, which in looking back seems about what I should have. You win some and lose some. This is especially the case in amateur boxing.

Even though I work exclusively as a psychiatrist, my experiences as a ringside physician and working with other amateur boxing officials allows me to attest to the safety of the sport. I also present information from other physicians who oppose boxing. Regarding safety, professional boxing is another matter. The risks associated with professional boxing are also presented, so it can be compared and contrasted with amateur boxing.

In addition to forging the mental strength to fight, amateur boxing offers other mental benefits. I present some of these benefits, which are transferable and have more value outside the ring. Also, through amateur boxing, I have met some people who have made me a better person. One of these was Randie Carver, and I write a little about my time with Randie.

Amateur boxing has taken me to various places I would not visit if it were not for boxing. One of these is Gleason's Gym in New York City where I competed in Gleason's International Masters Tournament in the summer of 2016. Walking into Gleason's Gym, you will see a large painting by American artist LeRoy Neiman (1921–2012) of two amateur boxers in the midst of their bout. The colors are vibrant and emanate action. Adjacent to this painting is a large sign with a quotation from the Roman poet, Virgil (70 BC–19 BC): "Now, whoever has courage, and a strong and collected spirit in his breast, let him come forward, lace on the gloves and put up his hands." These are inspiring words highlighted by Neiman's painting that would be appropriate in an art gallery, but much more appropriate being displayed at Gleason's Gym. In consideration of this, may the following words provide you direction to the appropriate venue for inspiration and action—your local boxing gym.

PART I
THE MENTAL STRESS OF BOXING

THE MENTAL COMBAT OF amateur boxing is hidden from the view of the audience during a bout. Nonetheless, it is quite a fight, a fight each boxer has already engaged in prior to physical combat. Before he steps into the ring, each boxer has had to have a tussle with the mental stress of boxing, that is, the negative emotions evoked by the bout. This is the first opponent you will face before the one you meet later on in the ring. Even though you are an individual, shaped by your own beliefs and experiences, every boxer experiences this same mental stress, which is a normal reaction to danger. These are the same negative emotions we all experience when faced with danger.

The response we all have to danger is embedded in our brain and body. This is a response with old evolutionary roots and has many components that are automatically implemented once danger has been detected. It has two components. One is fear, which is also known as the fight or flight response. Fear is not a voluntary response and will emerge when anyone encounters danger. Thus, fear affects *every* boxer. Everyone who has first ever stepped into the ring has been scared. If you have heard otherwise from a boxer, you have had a conversation with a liar. Fear, however, is not just triggered to scare the boxer. Fear also triggers a cascade of physiologic events that promote energy and awareness. This aspect of fear is beneficial to the boxer.

The second component of the mental stress of boxing is the anxiety that precedes the bout. This is called anticipatory anxiety, and it occurs as the boxer is preparing for and anticipating his bout.

This component responds more to reason than fear, but will last much longer and be more grueling than the fear encountered in the ring. Anticipatory anxiety also has benefits for the boxer. It serves as a catalyst to train effectively in preparation for the bout.

As such, this mental stress, your first opponent, is not just an adversary. This opponent can be used to your advantage. You can transform this mental stress of fear and anticipatory anxiety into mental strength. This requires mental preparation and strategy, well beyond physical preparation.

Physically, following a standard boxing training regimen will get you in shape. By and large, your muscles are biologically the same as everyone's muscles. A standard boxing regimen is not individualized for each boxer. Proper methods to develop punching strength and dexterity are well-established. These types of exercises can be done as a group or individually. The exercise needed to box is best expressed by Muhammad Ali (1942–2016) when asked about sit-ups; "Start counting when they start hurting, because those are the ones that count." But what do you count when trying to develop the mental strength to box? What exercises do you do to develop mental strength? These questions demonstrate how the mental preparation diverges from the physical preparation.

PART I: THE MENTAL STRESS OF BOXING

The first component of mental preparation is hand in hand with physical preparation. This preparation is the same for every boxer in training. Initially, most mental effort is devoted to learn basic boxing. As this is learned, less mental effort is expended on basic boxing and more is expended on advanced boxing. This stage utilizes the mental stress of boxing to learn to box correctly. This methodology also alleviates this mental stress. With progress in training, mentally you are not burdened by negative emotions. The negativity is replaced with calmness and determination to box well in preparation and during the bout. This is a demonstration of mental strength.

But this is not enough. Mental preparation requires a second component that addresses each boxer as an individual. Your response to the mental stress of boxing will be influenced by who you are and your experiences. Your brain is a much more sophisticated structure than your bicep muscle. You will react somewhat differently to mental stress than your fellow boxer. How you mentally prepare for your own unique response to fear and anticipatory anxiety will best be determined by you.

You will have to figure out what to count and what exercises to engage. I cannot tell you what is best for you. However, we both share a common opponent. All boxers, especially at the novice stage, experience the same mental stress. Facing and engaging this opponent allows you to find out what is best for you. To start this process, consider following the well-known advice of the ancient Chinese general, Sun Tzu, "Know the enemy and know yourself."

You need to know your opponent. Knowledge of the inner workings of fear and anticipatory anxiety provides you with some familiarity with the mental stress you are experiencing. Instead of just being scared, you, the informed boxer, will understand that your reaction is normal and predictable. You will not be overwhelmed by your internal sensations. Also, understanding what is happening in your brain and body, and the subsequent events that are triggered by amateur boxing, best prepares you to compete to your potential. You can now better and more easily transform this mental stress to mental strength.

Obviously, the mental stress of amateur boxing is internal, but this is no limitation. Your mental stress can be examined, explained, and understood. Neuroscience provides an appreciation of this mental stress. It offers an explanation and makes tangible what you cannot see, but which you can surely feel.

Neuroscience provides valuable insight into the mental stress of boxing, specifically the brain's response to danger. Since this is based on danger, you deserve to know what you are getting yourself into.

ONE
BOXING, THE SPORT

Born Fighters

IN THE PROFESSIONAL RANKS, it is not uncommon to hear a boxer claim that he is a "born fighter." Whether we are boxers or not, we are all born fighters. This is demonstrated soon after leaving the womb.

Infants in distress, such as those with colic, will clench their hands to make a fist and swing until restrained or calm. Infant fist clenching is observed throughout cultures and is a universal phenomenon. No matter the infant's upbringing, from Austria to Zimbabwe, an upset infant will make a fist and attempt to use it. The colicky newborn's fist clenching is a normal reaction to distress.

Also, universally observed is that infants do not slap when in distress. Biomechanical analysis reveals that compared to an open-handed slap, a fist transmits double the force. Additionally, a fist is safer, in that there is less risk to break a bone compared to an open hand. The fist is the body's weapon of choice (see Figure 1.1). With the clenched fist, and without any spoken words, the upset infant is able to fluently and efficiently communicate distress.

We come preprogrammed, so to speak, with the innate ability to inflict damage by punching with our fists. We probably have been using this ability from the get-go. For the first humans, this ability was probably necessary for protection.

Figure 1.1: The Fist, The Body's Weapon

With the development of tools, and subsequent weapons, fist fighting becomes less of a necessity for survival. However, as humans lived in larger groups, the use of one's fists to resolve conflict within the group most likely emerged. Samples of prehistoric skeletal remains reveal facial skeletal trauma consistent from injury due to fist fighting.

This type of conflict resolution is still seen today. For example, young children sometimes resort to punching when words are not enough to determine whose turn is it to go down the slide at the playground. Children also have keen sense of fairness, especially when they perceive they are not being treated fairly. This concept of fairness most likely was also appreciated by early man. Therefore, it is a reasonable hypothesis to speculate that boxing, the sport, gradually emerged in antiquity as a contest to determine the victor in a fair fight.

History

While the genesis of boxing is pure speculation, archaeological images depict boxing throughout Mesopotamia and the Mediterranean from the third millennium BC. Ancient Greece, with its plethora of art and writings available for contemporary study, provides many examples of boxing. For example, Homer's *Iliad* describes boxing during the Trojan War, and boxing was a component of the ancient Olympic games. Boxing continued during the Roman Empire, and then declined during the Dark and Middle Ages. More lethal competitions with swords, lances, quarterstaffs, etc., were popular at that time.

After the arrival of the Renaissance, with the development of an appreciation that life need not be nasty, brutish, and short and contests between men need not be lethal, boxing reemerged in England. By the eighteenth century, rules that provided a standard of fair play were implemented. In 1867, introduction of the Queensberry Rules, named so as they were endorsed by the Marquess of Queensberry, provided further rules to protect the boxers. These same rules are used today, such as mandatory gloves, ten seconds time to recover from a knockdown, and timed rounds and rest.

The safety measures provided with the adoption of the Queensberry rules are what drove the expansion of amateur boxing. The Amateur Boxing Association of England was formed in 1880 for the encouragement and development of boxing solely for the benefits of the sport itself. Shortly thereafter, national governing bodies formed in other countries, with the Amateur Athletic Union (AAU) forming in the United States in 1888 with boxing as one of its original sports. In 1946, the Association Internationale de Boxe Amateur, now named AIBA International Boxing Association was created to regulate amateur boxing worldwide. Currently, USA Boxing, a descendant of the AAU, is the authoritative agency that governs amateur boxing in the United States. USA Boxing monitors hundreds of boxing clubs throughout the country. These clubs have registered amateur boxing programs, certified coaches, and officials. USA Boxing is the gateway for amateur boxers who aspire to enter the Olympic Games.

Rules

Boxing today has not strayed far from the Queensberry rules for both amateur and professional boxing. Boxers are matched according to their weight. No consideration is given for height or build. Each individual round is not more than three minutes, with a rest break of a minute between rounds. In both, each boxer

BOXING, THE SPORT

is assigned a corner, traditionally a blue or red corner that are diagonally opposite of each other. The other two corners, also diagonally opposite each other, are referred to as neutral corners and have no color assigned to them. (see Figure 1.2)

Your assigned corner is where you go to rest between rounds. This corner is where your seconds, which are the people who are there to assist you, such as your coach, provide instruction. The neutral corners are used as a location to house a boxer, while his opponent is being attended to by an official. As for officials, there are administrators, announcers, clerks, timekeepers, judges, physicians, and referees. The referee is the official in the ring who enforces the rules. Punches that score land on the face, side of the head, and trunk. Punches that are blocked by gloves and arms do not score. Punches below the waistline (the belt of the boxing

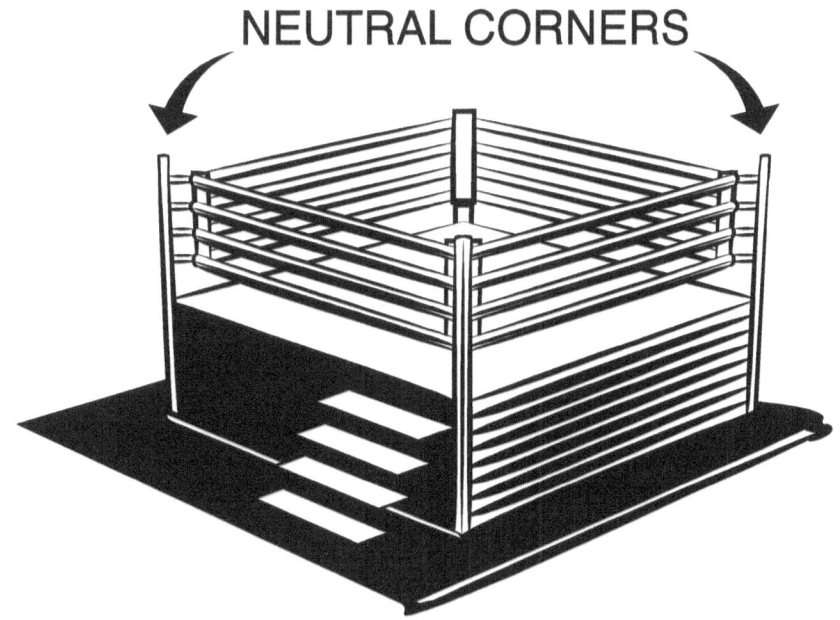

Figure 1.2: The Boxing Ring

trunks), and the top and back of the head are illegal. Only punches matter. There is no kicking, grasping, or wrestling allowed.

As for winning and scoring a bout in the both amateur and professional boxing, other than a knockout (KO) where the boxer fails to get up and/or continue after ten seconds of being knocked down, the determination is somewhat subjective. The factors considered in evaluating a boxer's performance are scoring punches, effective aggressiveness (initiating successful punches), defense (avoiding being punched), and ring generalship (controlling the action in the bout). (see Table 1.1) Multiple judges determine the winner of each round and, in most jurisdictions, follow the "10-Point Must System." In this system, ten points are awarded to the winner of the round, and nine or less are awarded to the loser. The score can be further revised by deducting points for infractions of the rules, which are termed fouls. The referee will make a determination during a round if a foul warrants a point deduction. If so, he will halt the bout. He then notifies the judges and spectators of the point deduction. Also, many amateur bouts are scored with the judges just determining the winner of the round and that boxer receives one point. The scores are tallied at the end of the bout. Also, the referee, ringside physician, and/or the seconds can stop the bout for the safety of the boxer. Such a decision is referred to as a technical knockout (TKO) in the professional ranks, and in the amateurs, a referee stops contest (RSC).

Table 1.1: The Four Factors to Judge Performance

- Scoring Punches
- Effective Aggressiveness
- Defense
- Ring Generalship

Amateur vs. Professional Boxing

At first sight, the difference between amateur and professional boxing is noting the different uniforms. Amateur boxers must wear a sleeveless shirt of a different color from the waistband of the trunks. Professional boxers do not wear shirts. However, looking closer beyond the uniforms, the difference between amateur and professional boxing is even more stark. Money is the fulcrum that splits professional boxing from amateur boxing. Professional boxing is a profession. Success in this profession requires a paying audience at the gate, viewing a screen, purchasing merchandise, and/or supporting businesses that endorse the boxers. The focus then of professional boxing is the audience. The spectator keeps the professional boxer working.

That people pay to view professional boxing is understandable. The level of proficiency is tremendous at the highest levels. Professional boxers make hard tasks look easy and bring an artistry to their work. Furthermore, they are able to sustain this ability for an extended period of time. The number of rounds boxed in a professional boxing match ranges from four rounds for beginning professional boxers and continues in even numbered increments to the maximum of twelve rounds for championship bouts. Commensurate with their professionalism, the pay for professional boxers at the highest levels is lucrative. Their abilities are top-notch. When two boxers of the highest caliber meet in the ring, the bout can be appreciated as high art, an art which is both brutal and exhilarating. People appreciate and pay for such art.

Professional boxing is a spectacle, because the audience also views and understands what is at stake. The job is dangerous with a real risk of death. The professional boxer and the audience both know of this risk. While medical supervision and intervention lower this risk, it is not eliminated. This is high stakes for the professional boxer. Also, from a monetary standpoint, the pay is terrible for lower- and middle-rung professional boxers. In these professional stages, many boxers need to support themselves and their families with additional jobs. Advancement or the lack of advancement can have a significant impact on a professional boxer's income. There can be much money at stake on the outcome of one bout for the professional boxer.

The money involved also has an impact on who boxes whom, which is referred to as matchmaking. In professional boxing, there are a multitude of sanctioning bodies that rank professional boxers on ability. These rankings provide a rough estimate of merit and provide a basis for matchmaking, but the overall determining factor in matchmaking is financial. Whatever matchmaking brings in the most money or largest audience is the correct one. This can lead to matches between boxers of differing proficiency, referred to as a mismatch when addressing the skill of the boxers alone.

Amateur boxing lacks this financial influence because the vast majority of boxers are never going to make a job out of it and become professional boxers. The focus is on the boxer, so he can get the most out of the sport. Because the focus is on the boxer, fairness and safety of the bout are paramount.

In amateur boxing, every attempt is made to have a fair bout. Matchmaking is based on experience and win-loss records. Advancement within amateur tournaments is based on merit. The goal is to have bouts between boxers of equal ability. Mismatches are avoided. What this leads to, as a mathematical fact, is that almost all amateur boxers lose at some time. In amateur boxing, the bouts consist of three rounds where three judges score the bout. Each judge must determine a winner of each round. As three is an odd number, each judge will have a score that favors one boxer over the other in the bout. Also, as there are three judges, the same math applies. It is mathematically impossible to have a tie, only a winner and loser. (To note, there are extremely rare cases in amateur boxing where point deductions for fouls come into play. This can lead to a tie, which is referred to as a "draw" in boxing. This contrasts to professional boxing where the bouts are in even-numbered increments, and draws are prevalent.) This means that half of the boxers who enter an amateur boxing show that day or evening will lose. And most amateur boxers who enter a multiday tournament will end the tournament with a loss.

Losing is normal in amateur boxing and is considered a learning experience. All elite amateur boxers have lost at some time. One cannot learn and get better if not tested by strong opposition. For example, Floyd J. Mayweather (1977–), who retired with fifty professional boxing wins and no losses, lost multiple times as an amateur boxer. His professional success, in part, was due to the experience he had as an amateur boxer.

Losing is part and parcel with participation in amateur boxing. So is safety. Amateur boxing officials, first and foremost, maintain the safety of the boxers. Officials must stop a bout if there is any concern for the well-being of a boxer. Safeguards are the physician, the referee, and each boxer's seconds. From my experience as a ringside physician, I would stop a bout if I had a thought of potential injury. Never mind waiting for my findings upon examination. While a stopped contest is unpopular with the boxer and sometimes his family, this is the policy of physicians and officials in amateur boxing.

An additional safety measure that is used in amateur boxing and no longer used in professional boxing is the "standing eight-count," which can be considered similar to a timeout in other sports. A standing eight-count is when the referee temporarily stops the bout when a boxer is not protecting himself and is in danger of harm. The boxer is given an eight-second respite. In theory, the bout is ended after three standing eight-counts, but in practice, the standing eight-count is used as an official warning to the boxer. The bout is usually stopped after two of these warnings.

The gloves used in amateur boxing are another safeguard. Based on the weight class, the gloves are larger and heavier compared to ones worn by professional boxers. This allows more padding over the fist, which protects the hands. Larger gloves also lessen the efficiency of the fist, as a harder punch can be delivered with a smaller glove. Last, headgear is used in amateur boxing during competition. Headgear is used by both amateur and professional boxers when practicing. It is debatable if headgear offers protection from the impact of a punch, but headgear clearly protects the boxer from facial and head injuries, such as cuts. Facial and head cuts are more significant injuries in amateur boxing compared to professional boxing. Amateur boxing tournaments take place over days or weeks. There is no time for a cut to heal, and such an injury can prevent medical clearance for the winning boxer to advance. Professional boxing tournaments are not that common. When they do occur, they are held over months, which is enough time for a boxer to heal from a cut.

While headgear is protective, in 2013, AIBA International Boxing Association lifted the requirement for headgear for elite adult amateur males. Headgear is still used in amateur competition for youth, female, and Masters boxers. Also, in 2016, professional boxers were allowed to participate in the Olympic games. These actions blur the distinction between amateur and professional boxing. Nonetheless, headgear is a safeguard that is used by both amateur and professional boxers.

Medical Risks of Injury and Death

One does not need to be a physician to understand that getting punched in the head is not healthy. Within the skull, the brain is protected not only by the hard bone of the skull, but also by cerebrospinal fluid. Cerebrospinal fluid is a cushion between the brain and skull that is a shock absorber for head trauma. Getting hit hard in the head can exceed the ability of the cerebrospinal fluid to protect the brain, and the brain can be jostled about within the skull. This action can cause a concussion, which is a temporary loss of brain function.

The loss of brain function in a concussion can vary. Headaches and problems concentrating are predominant symptoms of a mild concussion. A severe concussion can impair memory and coordination. Also, a severe concussion can present as a temporary loss of consciousness.

Concussions are common, with one in four Americans experiencing a concussion sometime during their life. Most people who suffer from a concussion will regain full brain function soon after the concussion. By definition, a concussion is temporary. However, about a quarter of people will still suffer prolonged symptoms of concussion. This is referred to as "post-concussion syndrome," where symptoms can last over three months.

Amateur boxing has strict rules regarding concussions. If a boxer has suffered a mild concussion in sparring or competition, he is automatically restricted from boxing for the next thirty days. This includes training, as well as the expected sparring and competition. Also, this boxer is required to undergo medical evaluation after the thirty days. His medical clearance requires that he be free of any concussion symptoms. For a severe concussion that presents with a loss of consciousness, the automatic restriction is ninety to one-hundred-and-eighty days.

Recovering fully from a concussion is important. If an individual still has lingering symptoms of concussion and receives head trauma, he is more apt to suffer another concussion. Repeated concussions are dangerous. The subsequent concussion can be more severe and persistent. Recovery tends to take more time. Also, repetitive concussions can lead to permanent brain injury.

The risk of permanent brain injury and death in boxing has been studied by physicians. The findings are expected and follow common sense. The phrase "punch drunk" first entered the medical literature in 1928 in the Journal of the American Medical Association. Here, American forensic pathologist Harrison S. Martland (1883–1954) described a condition particular to professional boxers, which he termed punch drunk. Interestingly, he borrowed this phrase from a boxing expression for a damaged fighter. For the modern reader interested in 1920s boxing parlance, Dr. Martland also provides synonyms such as "cuckoo," "goofy," "cutting paper dolls," and "slug nutty."

While Dr. Martland's addition of punch drunk to medical nomenclature has been replaced with other terms such as dementia pugilistica and now chronic traumatic encephalopathy (CTE), his description was prescient. (see Figure 1.3) He noted slow speech, movement, and tremor that in many cases were mild. Also noted were later stages and symptoms that mimicked those seen in Parkinsonian diseases. Describing the afflicted, Dr. Martland wrote, "Punch drunk most often affects fighters of the slugging type, who are usually poor boxers and who take considerable head punishment, seeking only to land a knockout blow. It is also common in second rate fighters used for training purposes, who may be knocked down several times a day. Frequently it takes a

PUNCH DRUNK

DEMENTIA PUGILISTICA

CHRONIC TRAUMATIC ENCEPHALOPATHY (CTE)

Figure 1.3 Prior Nomenclature for CTE

fighter from one to two hours to recover from a severe blow to the head or jaw. In some cases, consciousness may be lost for a considerable period of time."

Dr. Martland proposed an etiology to the condition, which is very similar to what is known now. Strong punches, such as to the chin which then acts as a fulcrum to rapidly jar the head, can cause the brain to hit against the skull, exceeding the protection offered by cerebrospinal fluid. Dr. Martland proposed that this type of repeated head trauma causes microhemorrhages (small bleeding within the brain) and these hemorrhages are replaced with gliosis (brain scar tissue). This progressive gliosis is what then leads to a boxer becoming punch drunk.

While the role of microhemorrhages in the development of punch drunk, now referred to as CTE, is not established, the formation of what can be considered brain scar tissue is. CTE is associated with the accumulation and aggregation of tau proteins, whose normal function is to provide stability to brain tissue. This pathology can only be detected by histologic examination of a slice of brain tissue via a microscope. Therefore, CTE can only be diagnosed by autopsy after death. Even though CTE cannot be definitively diagnosed in a living patient, having a history of repeated head trauma and progressive neurological and, at times, psychological decline lends to a strong suspicion of the diagnosis. CTE is a serious condition. There is no cure or effective treatment, and the only remedy is to prevent further head trauma.

CTE is now recognized as afflicting many participants of sports with head injuries, such as football, ice hockey, and even soccer players who frequently head the ball. There is ongoing study of CTE in these sports, as well as boxing. For example, The Professional Fighters Brain Health Study at the Cleveland Clinic Lou Ruvo Center for Brain Health in Las Vegas, Nevada, started in 2011, is a study of active professional fighters (boxers and mixed martial arts fighters) and retired professional fighters. The goal in this study is to evaluate the fighters' histories of head trauma with potential changes in brain imaging and physical and mental functioning over time. As the minimum period of study is five years and enrollment of fighters is ongoing, the final results are not in. However, prior studies have clearly shown the occupational hazards of professional boxing. The most extensive study was an evaluation of ex-professional boxers in Britain in the late 1960s who had boxed from 1929 through 1955. Seventeen percent of these boxers had symptoms of what now is considered CTE.

The risk of CTE, about one in five, is a significant occupational hazard for the professional boxer. Death is an additional hazard, and a real risk. The most thorough study evaluated boxing mortality from 1950 to 2007. During this time period, there were 339 deaths. Sixty-one percent occurred in the ring, the remaining in the locker room and outside the arena. Interestingly, this time period allowed evaluation of mortality after 1983, when championship bouts were reduced from fifteen to twelve rounds. One would think that this change, in itself, would led to a decrease in mortality. It has not. While there has been a decline in deaths over time, this decline is not related to a reduction in rounds. Most likely the decline in deaths is the result of less exposure to repetitive head trauma, since contemporary professional boxers have fewer bouts now compared to boxers in the 1950s.

It will be interesting to see if this same trend is found with CTE. Maybe there will be less risk of developing CTE compared to the early twentieth century. Contemporary studies should be able to answer this question and others in the next decade or so.

As for amateur boxing, there are no punch drunk amateur boxers. The safety measures of larger gloves, less rounds, standing eight-counts, strict rules regarding concussions, and the discouragement of mismatches all lead to less brain injury. Headgear may offer some minor protection against concussions or other brain injury, but this protection is not well-established. The other safeguards employed are much more important and protective.

With these safeguards, scientific scrutiny bears out what one would expect to find in amateur boxing. The vast majority of studies find no lasting injuries from head trauma. In the minority of studies that do, the quality of the evidence is poor which, to the researchers' credit, is typically admitted as so; (e.g., finding minor electroencephalogram [EEG, a test of electrical activity in the brain] dysfunction in amateur boxers.) Instead of this minor finding being a result of participation in amateur boxing, it could be transient, an artifact, or result of something other than amateur boxing. These types of findings are a weak foundation to make a conclusion that participation in amateur boxing leads to permanent brain damage. The significance given to such minor findings is further discounted when comparing these studies to studies of professional boxers, where there is clear evidence of traumatic and permanent brain damage.

However, there is risk of death in amateur boxing, though, this risk is so low and the direct connection to amateur boxing not clear, it is hard to take any meaning from it. From 1918 to 1983 there have been 190 boxing fatalities in amateur boxing worldwide. This seems like a significant number, but this number has to be placed in context of the number of amateur bouts during this time period. At a very low estimate, hundreds of thousands of amateur boxing matches have occurred worldwide over this time period. Considering the relatively low numbers of fatalities compared to the very high number of bouts, the risk is extremely low. For example, looking at soccer fatalities, an estimated 151 soccer-related deaths occurred in the United States from 2004–2013. Soccer is much more popular than amateur boxing, with over three million youths participating annually in the United States. Comparing a decade of soccer participation in the United States with almost seven decades of amateur boxing worldwide is reasonable for these purposes. Considering, again with a very low estimate, there have been hundreds of thousands of soccer matches in the United States during this time period, the risk of death playing soccer is extremely low.

Also, when an extremely rare fatality has occurred in amateur boxing, the circumstances of the fatality have been investigated. For example, over an eight-year period there were 180,000 participants in the instructional boxing component of US Marine Corps basic training. During this time period, two male Marine recruits succumbed to boxing-related deaths, though neither Marine reported prior head injury or concussions before the fatal incident, despite both having histories of such. These prior injuries have an impact on risk assessment, as it is difficult to determine how much of an effect the prior head trauma contributed to their deaths. Also, if they had reported their prior injuries, this would have been properly evaluated for medical clearance. They may not have been allowed to participate.

In view of the medical risks inherent in professional boxing, many medical organizations, such as the American Medical Association, have had long-standing position statements that recommend that boxing be banned. This is not out of the ordinary. Professional boxing is dangerous, and physicians have a responsibility to notify the public of health risks. Moreover, considering the risks, professional boxers have to be consenting adults to obtain a license, which in the United States is at age eighteen. Professional boxing licenses are issued and regulated by each individual state, but all states require medical clearance and informed consent.

There are significant risks of injury and death with professional boxing, but none of these same risks with amateur boxing. Yet, the lack of valid medical evidence has not dissuaded some physicians and physician organizations from adopting a policy that opposes amateur boxing. In 2011, The American Academy of Pediatrics and the Canadian Paediatric Society published a policy statement opposing boxing as a sport for children and adolescents, coupled with the recommendation that physicians encourage patients to participate in alternative sports in which intentional head blows are not central to the sport. From a personal and medical standpoint, this policy statement is surprising and invites closer scrutiny. After all, I was first introduced to amateur boxing by my pediatrician. As expected and true, the physicians generating this policy write of the risk of head and facial injuries. Also, correctly noted, is the lowered risk of injury in amateur boxing when compared to other amateur (high school) athletes in sports such as football, wrestling, and soccer. There are no subsequent policies to ban high school football, wrestling, and soccer, so the policy, perhaps, is based on the concept of intention of injury.

Intentional injury is not a component of amateur boxing. No amateur boxer goes in the ring wanting to hurt the other boxer and he expects the same courtesy from his opponent. You both want to walk out of the ring after the bout without injury. There is no glory or reward in injuring your opponent. For argument's sake, even if you are an evil boxer intent on injuring your opponent, in amateur boxing he will be at approximately the same level of skill as you, as there should be no mismatch. A bout between evenly matched boxers is less likely to lead to injury than a bout between mismatched boxers. Also, there are many safety measures implemented, as mentioned earlier, to prevent injury and officials at the bout enforce these measures. If you have intentions of injuring your opponent, the boxing ring is not the place to do this. The officials will not let you.

That these physicians would generate a policy statement without any significant medical evidence to support it is possibly based on their conceptualization and concern that intentional head blows are central to the sport. Ignoring the injury component, the concern of these physicians and others is understandable regarding intent. The intent of the amateur boxer is to literally beat his opponent. An amateur boxer is trained and encouraged to punch his opponent efficiently and repeatedly in the scoring areas of the head and body. Intentional head blows are essential to the sport.

While intentionally punching your opponent is essential in amateur boxing, it is not central to the sport. Your intention to punch your opponent is only one component of the sport. Amateur boxing is more than punching an opponent. While punching is essential, the whole of boxing takes into account that the intent of your opponent is to punch you. In other words, your opponent is not a punching bag. He can punch back. Intent is a two-way street in amateur boxing, and this intent is what makes boxing challenging and stressful.

A spectator may not have the same understanding of the intent of your opponent as you do being in the ring with him. The spectator's viewpoint is different than yours. (see Figure 1.4) The intent of your opponent is not a concept. His intent and actions are real. Your opponent's brain and body are as active as yours. You notice his eyes are watching you like a hawk. You recognize his intent and action as danger, and this evokes significant mental stress. The whole of amateur boxing includes this mental stress. Addressing this mental stress is essential to the sport. This will be a challenge for you, especially when you first feel it. These feelings are the fear and anticipatory anxiety of amateur boxing.

Figure 1.4: The Whole of Boxing: Your intentional head blow and your opponent's intent.

Two

THE NEUROSCIENCE OF FEAR

Take-Home Points

- Fear is essential for life.
- Fear emerges automatically when danger is present to protect you.
- Fear stimulates the brain and body for maximum performance.
- Fear allows you to respond quickly and accurately to danger, which is needed when you are in the ring.

Survival: The evolution of fear

FEAR IS NATURAL. SIMPLY, it is the sensations and behaviors evoked when danger is immediate or imminent. The physical sensations of rapid heartbeats, deep breathing, sweating, muscle tension, restlessness, and nausea are all associated with fear.

Additionally, psychological sensations such as heightened awareness and apprehension are evoked. The role of fear is to stimulate the body to appraise and survive danger, allowing one to perform maximally during a threatening situation. Fear fulfills an essential function for all in the animal kingdom. Life requires an ability to survive the danger that is ubiquitous for the living. Fear keeps us safe. Without fear, we would not recognize and protect ourselves from danger.

Essential to living, fear has a long history. Understanding the evolution of fear is helpful in understanding how fear manifests in us. The first life forms were the single-celled prokaryotes that emerged about 3.5 billion years ago. Prokaryotes and other single-celled organisms, then and now, and like us, have two basic states—activity and rest. During activity, referred to as a catabolic state, energy is generated for growth and reproduction. During rest, referred to as an anabolic state, energy is stored and components of the organism repaired. When the opportunities arise for activity, such as available food and temperature, bacteria seize these opportunities with growth and reproduction. Conversely, when opportunities are limited, bacteria can become dormant. This ability to become dormant offers resiliency for bacteria. It allows for conservation of energy when its use would not be productive. Also, dormancy offers protection from harm. For example, the antibiotic penicillin requires bacterial growth to be effective. Penicillin causes bacterial death by disrupting cellular activities involved in new cell wall formation needed for growth and reproduction.

While dormancy is a method for survival, it is not efficient. In other words, one cannot grow and reproduce if sleeping all the time. Bacteria have developed another mechanism for survival. They fight. As opposed to the dormancy state, bacteria utilize the catabolic pathway to respond to threats. The "bacterial stress response" is an active catabolic response of bacteria to environmental (outside) stressors. This is the precursor to fear in humans.

There are a variety of different responses of bacteria depending on the threat. Changes in temperature, acidity, electrolytes, etc., all trigger the bacterial stress response. This ability not only allows for bacterial survival, it also contributes to disease in humans. For example, Salmonellosis, an infection of the intestine that can be fatal in compromised patients, is caused by the prokaryotic bacterium *Salmonella enterica*. This bacterium is able to utilize the bacterial stress response in order to survive transit in food, usually poultry, and the acid in the stomach. Once past these barriers, the bacterium thrives in the intestine where it causes disease.

While the specific response of the bacterium depends on the threat encountered and the defense of bacterium available, the mechanism is essentially the same. The bacterium senses a danger to its survival outside, and transmits this warning to the interior of the cell where the bacterium can generate machinery and activity to counter the threat. "Signal transduction" is the mechanism by which the bacterium implements the stress response, and the significance for us is that this mechanism has persisted through evolution. (see Figure 2.1)

As life has evolved, signal transduction has been preserved as the mechanism for communication from the outside of the cell to the inside as organisms evolved from the simplest prokaryotes, to complex, multicelled organisms. It is estimated that a human has over 30 trillion cells, of many different types, all of which have to communicate in order to act together as a whole. Considering the almost inconceivable number and types of cells found in the human body, only a few types of signal transduction pathways are utilized.

Figure 2.1: Fear in Bacteria

These pathways evolved in part from a primordial need to actively fight for survival. Signal transduction allows the bacterium to implement its stress response to danger. It is an efficient way to communicate, and thus has been preserved through evolution to us. This communication, shaped by danger, is a part of who we are.

Additionally, natural selection, which in essence is an organism's response to danger over generations, has also shaped the bacterial stress response to what we have in us. As animals have evolved, the mechanisms to respond to danger have differentiated to sophisticated and specialized groups of cells that are better able to appraise and respond to threats.

This differentiation has provided a sophisticated system in humans that involves more than what is found in bacteria. Notable, in evolution, is the development of the nervous system in higher life forms, specifically the brain.

From the Stress Response to Fear

The human nervous system, which is how information is processed and communicated, has two parts. The central nervous system (CNS) is basically the brain and the spinal cord, where the individual brain cells are termed "neurons," and the peripheral nervous system (PNS), are primarily nerves found in the body. (There are some nerves within the peripheral nervous system that emerge directly from the brain and some of these do not reach the body. These are termed "cranial nerves," but still are considered part of the peripheral nervous system). Within the peripheral nervous system is a nervous system that is built upon its bacterial ancestors, the autonomic nervous system (ANS).

The autonomic nervous system, as its name implies, operates autonomously or unconsciously, that is without conscious thought. Like the two basic metabolic states found in bacteria, the ANS is divided into two opposing operating systems, the parasympathetic and sympathetic. The anatomy of the ANS is complex, but all of the nerves emerge from the brain and spinal cord to exert their effects on the body. (see Figure 2.2)

The parasympathetic system primarily uses the neurotransmitter acetylcholine to activate an anabolic response for rest and repair. For example, when the parasympathetic system is activated, heart rate and muscle activity are slowed and digestion is increased. The sympathetic system activates a catabolic state where the body is prepared for action. The sympathetic nervous system primarily uses the neurotransmitters, norepinephrine and epinephrine,

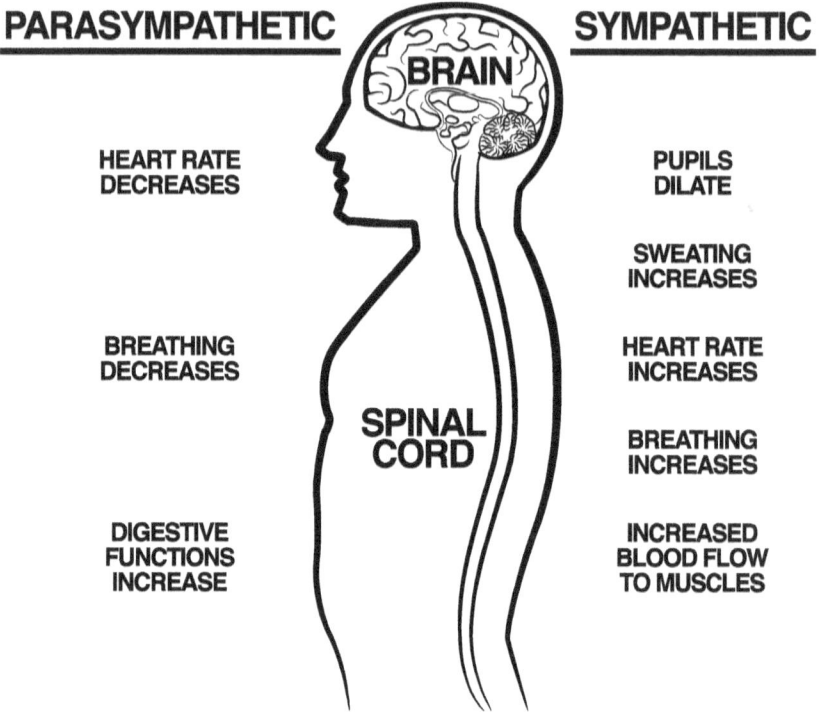

Figure 2.2: Autonomic Nervous System

commonly referred to as "adrenaline." The activated sympathetic nervous system increases physical activity necessary for action. Adrenaline causes our eyes to dilate in order to enhance vision, increases heart rate, breathing, blood flow to the muscles, awareness, and apprehension. This is the body's warm-up for action.

While the autonomic nervous system operates unconsciously, it can activate conscious areas of the brain. It was not until relatively recently – the twentieth century—that the connection between the brain and the sympathetic nervous system was explained. Harvard physician Walter B. Cannon, MD (1871–1945), incorporating his and others' studies from a variety of different experiments, formulated the first brain mechanism on how we respond to danger.

Dr. Cannon described how danger is perceived by the brain in an area called the thalamus. (see Figure 2.3) The thalamus is an area deep within the center of the brain that has connections with almost every other part of the brain. The primary role of the thalamus is to process sensory information in the brain. The thalamus can be conceptualized as a router, in that it sends signals from our senses, (e.g., eyes and ears), to other areas of the brain. Danger, for example being pushed and yelled at by a bully at recess, is detected by the senses (the input). This data is conveyed as danger and routed by the thalamus to the appropriate areas of the brain for analysis. Sensory information about the danger is simultaneously sent to the cerebral cortex and the hypothalamus. The cerebral cortex is the large gray area of the brain where conscious thought and analysis of the senses take place. The cerebral cortex is where fear is perceived mentally. The hypothalamus, a small area of the brain below the thalamus, is involved in the

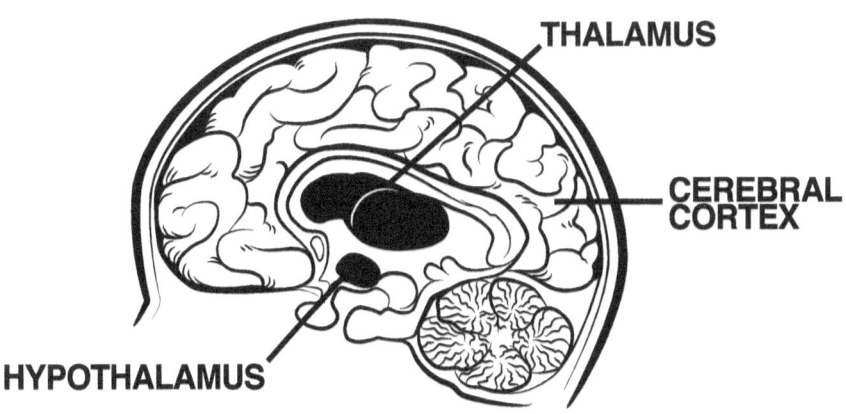

Figure 2.3: Anatomy of Thalamus, Hypothalamus, and Cerebral Cortex

regulation of the autonomic nervous system. Activation of the hypothalamus by danger stimulates the sympathetic nervous system and adrenaline is activated. In concert and automatically initiated, adrenaline activates the body for action and the brain is appraised of danger via the sensation of fear. (see Figure 2.4) As Dr. Cannon writes, "These are activities which in man are associated with attack or with flight from danger and are attended by the emotions of rage or fear." The "fight or flight" phrase came from his findings.

Dr. Cannon's work provided an understanding about how danger evokes both mental and physical reactions. Also, relying on examples from nature, the conflict between the predator and the prey, he demonstrated how his mechanism expressed itself in life. Simply, seizing prey and escaping from one's enemies requires both mental and physical effort. However, how this effort

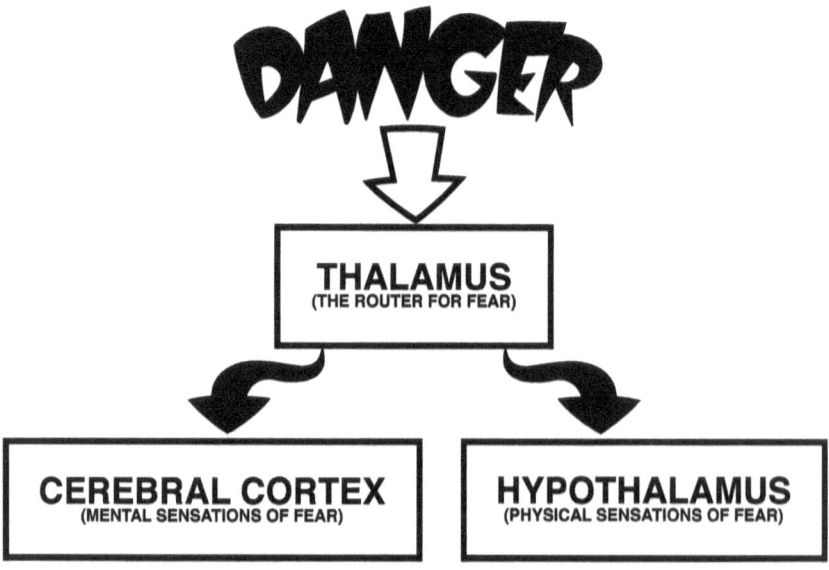

Figure 2.4: Schematic of Cannon's Mechanism of Fear

manifests in the brain exceeds Cannon's work. He was limited by the tools and understanding available at this time. Nonetheless, Dr. Cannon did have an appreciation of the fact that the correct decision for continued existence emerges from an assessment of danger from the brain.

Using the example of the bully, what is the correct decision? Maybe a strong punch to his nose is correct. Everyone is watching. If you do not stand up to him now, he will just do this again. Or possibly, a swift exit to the annex building. You may get punished more from your parents because of the likely suspension from school for fighting than anything he can dish out now. And you know he has it coming from other victims. He will get his soon enough. Obviously, the answer is not straight forward in humans confronted with danger. Human nature is complicated, and human fear mirrors this complexity.

Brain Development and Function in Fear

The complexity of human nature, from a neuroscience standpoint, is the development of the cerebral cortex. The cerebral cortex is the outermost and largest area of the brain where conscious thought arises. Simply looking at the brains of various animals, one can observe the increase in size of the cerebral cortex compared to other structures of the brain. (see Figure 2.5) In addition to the overall size of the cerebral cortex, comparing the gross anatomy of the cerebral cortex one clearly observes that the human brain is more wrinkled, compared to lower animals such as the rat. The human cerebral cortex is a convoluted organ in that the surface of the brain folds upon itself. The folds are termed "gyri," and the clefts between the folds are termed "sulci." The folding of cerebral cortex allows for a larger cortical surface area and also

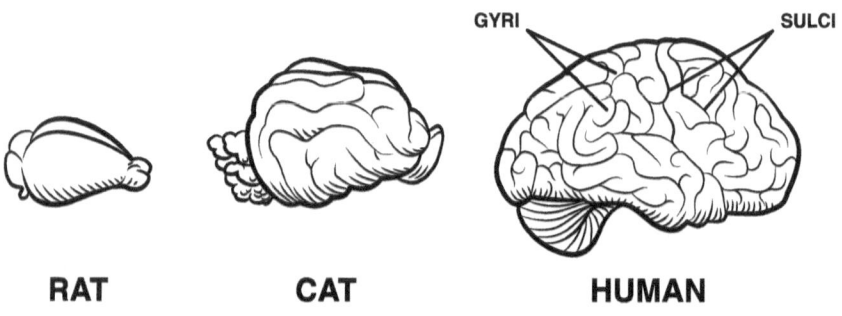

Figure 2.5: Evolution of the Cerebral Cortex

brings together areas of the cerebral cortex closer to one another. To make an analogy with a computer, this allows a larger, more powerful processor to be placed in a limited space and minimizes the wiring needed in the computer.

Like the advances seen in computing, the evolutionary gain of folding of the cerebral cortex allows more brain to fit within the confines of the skull and makes the brain circuitry more efficient. This provides more computational power, which in us is the heightened ability to think, imagine, and process information. As the cerebral cortex generates and processes these sophisticated functions and is literally higher and encases more primitive brain structures, it is referred to as "higher" in both structure and function compared to the deeper, primitive areas of the brain.

Human fear is impacted by the development of the cerebral cortex and other areas, with a degree of complexity and sophistication that was not apparent to Dr. Cannon. Dr. Cannon primarily relied on studies of animals, which was the standard of practice for his time. Modern medical research now has a number of tools, such as Magnetic Resonance Imaging (MRI). With MRI, brain function can be analyzed in living humans in a noninvasive and harmless manner. The neurochemistry of communication within the brain can be detected with such tools, and the biochemical workings understood with more precision.

The advances in research tools have had an impact on how neuroscience research is conducted. Simply, there are more tools available. This, in part, has contributed to "reductionism," which is the mainstay of how contemporary medical and scientific work is performed. Reductionism is the process of reducing a problem to its constituent parts and examining these parts individually. An example of applied reductionism is distributed computing. Distributed computing is the use of the processing power of many individual personal computers to create a supercomputer. Scientists who need to perform many calculations for their work, such as meteorologists who study global weather patterns, use this methodology.

In short, scientists who employ distributed computing divide the problem into different parts. These parts are then distributed to individual computers for processing. After many autonomous computers solve the small parts, the results are sent to back to the scientist for analysis. This reductionistic process allows the timely completion of complicated work, which would otherwise take years to perform.

Following the process of distributed computing, human fear is examined via reductionism. The brain mechanism(s) about how we respond to danger have been divided and distributed to many different fields. For example, researchers examine patients who have injuries to specific brain regions to determine what deficits arise, examine responses in humans and animals when exposed to a fear-evoking stimulus, look at brains with functional neuroimaging techniques to detect changes in brain function during fear, etc. Researchers from all over the world have approached the understanding of fear by applying their respected expertise to small parts of the problem. Also, one of the catalysts to this research is that many psychiatric conditions such as anxiety disorders have symptoms similar to fear that arise spontaneously or are produced out of proportion to what should be expected. The study of these conditions provides a better understanding of the brain mechanisms that give rise to normal and pathological fear.

As there are many researchers involved in this work, and the work is wide-ranging, it is challenging to ascribe one person or group of researchers to being the ones who have delineated how the brain functions during fear. Moreover, science is characterized by repetition of demonstrable facts. Experiments need to be repeated by others to be considered valid. This leads to many contributors and provides a tremendous body of information that advances neuroscience research. The credit for this advancement is shared among many.

Since Dr. Cannon outlined the first brain mechanism about how we respond to danger, the understanding of fear has included interactions of areas of the brain involved with emotions and memory. Also, the speed and quality of communication between areas of the brain during fear is now quantifiable. This work has shown the conscious areas of the brain in the cerebral cortex are not only notified of the danger, but also provide input to accurately access the danger in order to revise the response, if needed.

One of the contemporary contributors is New York University psychologist, Joseph E. LeDoux, PhD (1949–) and his colleagues. Dr. LeDoux's work has outlined the role of brain areas reappraising the initial sensations of fear so they can be revised. Moreover, these contributions are especially applicable to boxing, as this line of neuroscience research confirms what experienced boxers and their trainers already know—one reacts before one can think about doing so.

Dr. LeDoux's work has focused on the role of the amygdala and how it is involved with fear as well as anxiety disorders. The amygdala, literally derived from the Greek word for almond, is two almond-shaped areas deep within the brain that are mirror images of each other. The amygdala is a primitive area of the brain that first emerged with mammals. (see Figure 2.6)

The amygdala is considered a hub in the human stress response as it is central in the propagation of fear. When danger is imminent, the thalamus routes sensory information to the cerebral cortex for analysis. At the same time, as it is routing this sensory

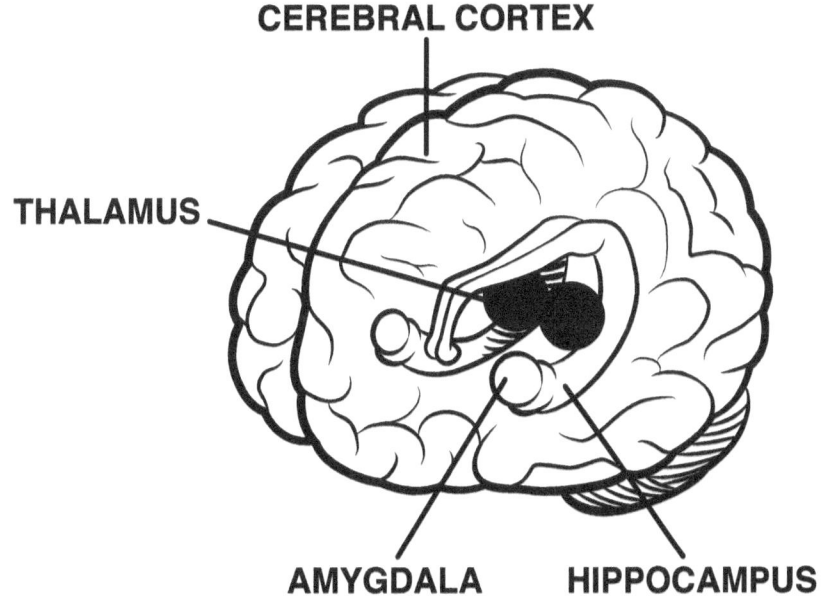

Figure 2.6: Anatomy of Amygdala and other Brain Structures in Fear

information to the cerebral cortex, the thalamus sends fast and primitive signals of this danger to the amygdala. This is considered the "fast track" of fear. (see Figure 2.7)

As the amygdala is part of the primitive brain, there is no conscious awareness of what the danger is, but it is recognized as danger, nonetheless. This can be considered an SOS signal to the amygdala. Like the Morse code for "save our ship," this signal to the amygdala is a simple and fast means by which to convey, "Danger is here. Help is needed." The amygdala, in turn, via a variety of brain circuits, activates the sympathetic nervous system for action. This generates the initial sensations of fear.

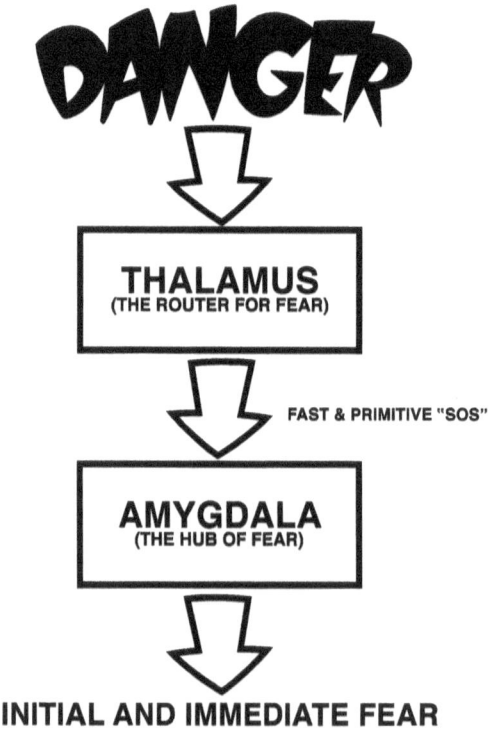

Figure 2.7: Schematic of Fast Track of Fear

THE NEUROSCIENCE OF FEAR

What this manifests physically is one being suddenly surprised or frightened; for example, being startled when walking into your room and seeing a man at your desk. Immediately you stop, your muscles tense, your eyes widen, and you possibly even jump back. These automatic behaviors are a function of an activated amygdala, and are independent of conscious thought.

Being a hub, the amygdala has communication with many areas of the brain that modulate fear. For example, the amygdala communicates with the hippocampus. The hippocampus is another primitive area of the brain that curves like a seahorse—the name derives from the Greek name for seahorse. The hippocampus is involved in the formation of memory, and its role in fear is to compare the danger to a memory or context. The amygdala also connects with the cerebral cortex, so the threat can be consciously appraised. The actions of the amygdala therefore are revised and regulated after the initial SOS signal has been sent. (see Figure 2.8)

When you have time to think, you also have time to assess the danger. As such, within moments after your fear arose, you recognize that this man is your brother. He is using your desk to get some work done, which he asked to do before he visited for the weekend.

While the brain areas and circuitry involved are more complex than presented here, stepping back and looking at the neuroscience of fear, the inner workings follow common sense. Danger is a normal part of life and needs to be recognized quickly. The initial SOS signal propagated by the amygdala is smart. Danger is danger. Using primitive structures that have persisted and been effective through evolution makes sure the signal is communicated without disruption. That fear presents as an immediate response to danger, even before we can even think about it, ensures an

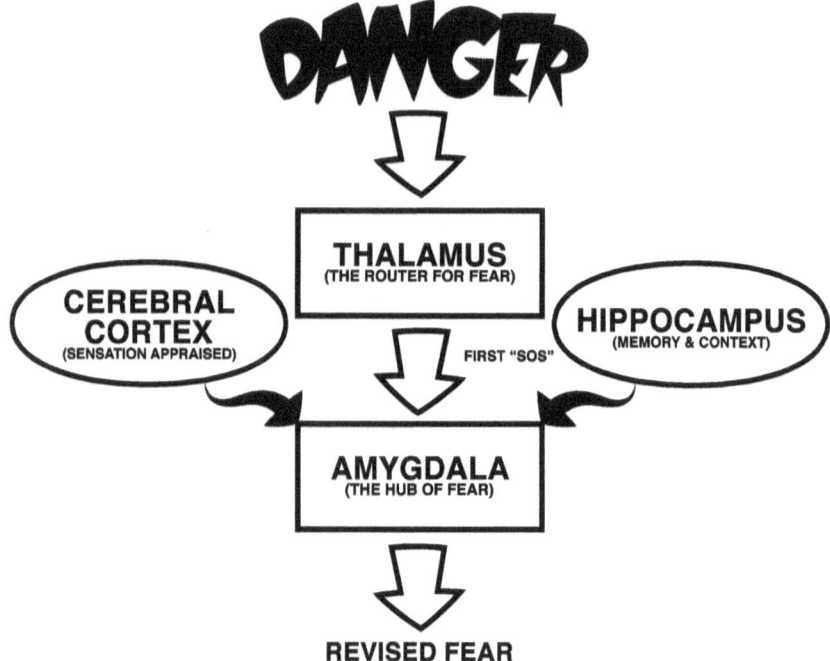

Figure 2.8: Schematic of Slow Track of Fear

immediate reaction. Obviously, we have an advanced brain so we might as well use these structures. That the amygdala is regulated by its connections with other areas of the brain, and seeks consultations about danger, results in a more accurate appraisal and response. In short, the two-track brain circuitry of fear is good. It allows us to respond quickly and accurately to danger, which is needed when you are in the ring.

Three
THE NEUROSCIENCE OF ANTICIPATORY ANXIETY

Take-Home Points

- Anticipatory anxiety prepares you for danger.
- Anticipatory anxiety is a negative emotion that forces you to evaluate or avoid danger.
- The negativity of anticipatory anxiety is lowered with sound mental and physical preparation.
- Anticipatory anxiety allows you to strengthen your brain and body to box better.

Anticipatory Anxiety: "Be prepared"

"BE PREPARED" IS THE motto of the Boy Scouts. From the Tenderfoot to the Eagle Scout, it is a concept fixed in scouting. Boy

Scouts are expected to anticipate and prepare for any challenges they might encounter while camping, earning merit badges, etc. As a proud Eagle Scout, I look back on this teenage accomplishment with fondness and an appreciation that it was achieved with much effort expended on planning and preparation.

To be prepared, one has to assess what is needed in the future and be ready. Preparedness makes challenges less of a challenge and leads to successful outcomes.

Nature also recognizes the effectiveness of preparation. When it comes to human nature and the assessment of danger, the brain has mechanisms that allow one to prepare before the danger is imminent. This type of preparation requires forethought, which means the cerebral cortex. Lower life forms do not have this ability to prepare for danger. For example, a Salmonella bacterium residing in undercooked chicken does not prepare itself before being ingested by a person to manufacture the protective proteins to survive the acidity of the human stomach. It is lacking the ability to anticipate the danger residing in the stomach.

We, however, do have this ability to prepare for danger. The feelings evoked to spur preparation are referred to as anticipatory anxiety. Anticipatory anxiety is the term used by psychiatrists and other mental health professionals to describe the normal feelings and behaviors that occur when danger is uncertain or distant. Accurately named, it is the mental state associated with the anticipation of danger. Anticipation anxiety is inherently a future-oriented mental state. As such, the time in this state is highly variable. Anticipatory anxiety emerges when the danger is recognized. It then persists until the danger has been avoided or becomes a certainty and is upon us. Far from being an instantaneous reaction, as in fear, anticipatory anxiety waxes and wanes over an extended period of time.

THE NEUROSCIENCE OF ANTICIPATORY ANXIETY

Anticipatory anxiety has a specific meaning from a mental health standpoint. Unfortunately, there are many words, such as panic, worry, nervousness, etc. both used medically and by the layperson interchangeably when describing anticipatory anxiety or fear. This leads to confusion as to what is being described, and that possibly these sensations are mental illness. Not so. Fear and anticipatory anxiety are normal reactions. The mental stress experienced in boxing is a normal reaction. In contrast, pathological anxiety of anxiety disorders, such as seen in panic attacks, arises spontaneously or is produced out of proportion to what should be expected.

Brain Function in Anticipatory Anxiety

Fear has been with us since the beginning of life. Anticipatory anxiety has not. There is not a clear evolutionary pathway for anticipatory anxiety like there is for fear. The genesis of anticipatory anxiety most likely mirrors the development of the cerebral cortex. The cerebral cortex is where imagination, sensation, movement, language, and thinking reside. All these functions are tools that can be used to accurately anticipate danger, so one can be best prepared for it.

Anticipatory anxiety primarily relies on the cerebral cortex. It utilizes these higher areas of our brain, and the neuroscience of the inner workings is extremely complex. From a circuitry standpoint, as described earlier, the cerebral cortex folds upon itself. This folding allows the different areas to be strongly interlinked.

Moreover, the cerebral cortex is highly interconnected with the primitive areas of the brain involved in fear. While anticipatory anxiety and fear are two different mental states, with anticipatory anxiety utilizing more of the cerebral cortex and fear primarily based in primitive brain areas, neuroscience research reveals there is some overlap in the brain circuitry of each. The inherent complexity of the brain circuitry alone observed in anticipatory anxiety exceeds current neuroscience tools for a full understanding of the definitive brain mechanisms that mediate the state.

Anticipatory anxiety is enmeshed in the complex circuitry of the cerebral cortex, which is made even more complex by the fact that this circuitry is more amenable to change than the primitive brain structures that mediate fear. The circuitry of the cerebral cortex is considered "plastic." Brain plasticity is the ability of the brain to change in response to environmental and psychological stimuli. In other words, the brain can change its own anatomy and function, its circuitry, in response to what is encountered and what tasks are performed. For example, the plasticity of the cerebral cortex allows one to learn. Teaching stimulates neurons in the brain, and these stimulated neurons will recruit other neurons to join them. Repeated neuronal stimulation will promote further connections. The molecular process that leads to long lasting neuronal change is termed, "long-term potentiation." The exact mechanisms for long-term potentiation are not yet delineated, but it is well established that this process contributes to the long-lasting changes in the anatomy and function of the brain to understand and perform what is being taught. As brain plasticity relates to anticipatory anxiety, your experiences influence how anticipatory anxiety manifests in you. Compared to fear, anticipatory anxiety is a mental state that is more dependent on the individual than the species as a whole.

While the neuroscience of the inner workings of anticipatory anxiety are complex, it does not mean that it is unknown. Stepping back, anticipatory anxiety is simple in function, and there are some basic tenets of the neuroscience involved that have been worked out.

THE NEUROSCIENCE OF ANTICIPATORY ANXIETY

It is understood that anticipatory anxiety is evoked and reinforced by negative associations. This is in contrast to many other essential functions, which are mediated in the brain by positive associations. For example, essential behaviors such as sex and eating utilize a reward circuit that evokes pleasurable feelings. At first blush, one would think that nature should have incorporated this reward pathway for anticipatory anxiety. Since protecting oneself from danger seems to be as an essential function as sex and eating, why not have the preparation for such danger rewarded pleasurably? This might work, but nature has taken the course that the best preparation for danger is to avoid it. Hence anticipatory anxiety, as well as fear, are governed by negative feelings.

The negative associations of anticipatory anxiety are internally generated and can manifest as the same symptoms of fear. For example, mentally one can experience dread, vigilance, and sadness. Physical symptoms can present as muscle tension, sweating, and insomnia. While similar to feelings of fear, the negativity of anticipatory anxiety is not generated to address immediate danger. The role of this negativity is to spur us to evaluate the upcoming danger, then take mental and physical efforts to reduce the risk of experiencing the detrimental emotional or physical effects of the danger. Anticipatory anxiety, being negative, does not mean that it is bad.

The neuroscience of the negative associations that resemble fear in anticipatory anxiety is known. These are simply the same mechanisms utilized in fear. The cerebral cortex has direct connections with these primitive brain areas and activates them to stimulate our preparation. Other negative associations that can be present in anticipatory anxiety such as sadness and insomnia are mediated by different pathways within and outside the cerebral cortex.

Obviously, experiencing the same symptoms of fear is not helpful now. Danger is not immediate. The brain and body do not need to be activated for fight or flight at this stage. Moreover, the additional negative associations like sadness and insomnia are not advantageous. Being preoccupied with negativity is harmful when preparing for danger. These negative associations then have to be properly appraised to motivate helpful thoughts and behavior. The cerebral cortex does have a mechanism to address this negativity. The main brain structure in the cerebral cortex that controls the mechanism is the prefrontal cortex.

The prefrontal cortex is at the very front and one of the larger subregions of the cerebral cortex. (see Figure 3.1) Compared to other mammals, the human prefrontal cortex constitutes a much larger portion of the cerebral cortex. Size alone gives some insight into prefrontal cortex function. The cerebral cortex mediates functions that are thought to be specific to humans, which are commonly referred to as "executive functions." Executive functions include reasoning, abstract thought, judgment, and planning. Collectively these executive functions allow us to integrate what we experience in the world with what we know and think. These abilities,

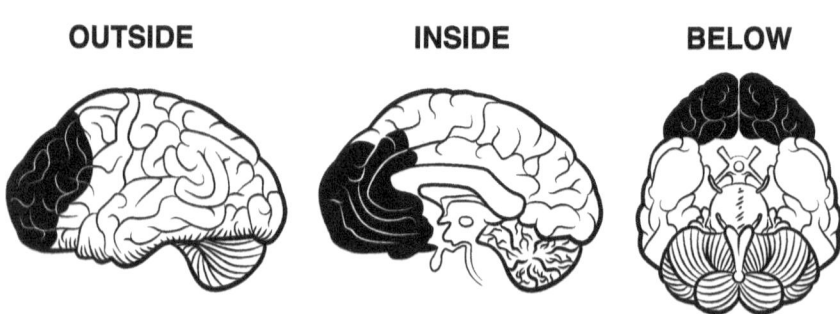

Figure 3.1: The Prefrontal Cortex

like reasoning and planning, allow us to pursue goal-directed behaviors.

Activation of the prefrontal cortex is one of the processes that occurs during anticipatory anxiety. The ability of the prefrontal cortex to intelligently pursue goals allows us to be best prepared for danger. This type of function requires attention. In order not to be distracted by the negativity evoked by anticipatory anxiety, the prefrontal cortex takes charge. The prefrontal cortex lowers the negative associations, while concurrently activating executive functions. There is no consensus on the definitive neuronal pathways. Current debate ranges over the importance of various structures of the brain areas involved and time is variable. However, activation of the prefrontal cortex clearly suppresses fear circuit activity.

The Neuronal Processing of Anticipatory Anxiety Compared to Fear

Neuroscientists refer to the ability of the prefrontal cortex to regulate the negative associations of anticipatory anxiety as "top-down" processing. Top-down processing is the use of higher brain areas to dictate responses. Anticipatory anxiety is a mental state that follows top-down processing. The cerebral cortex is primarily involved, and, therefore, our internal thoughts and knowledge are as significant as the external potential danger that is to be addressed. This is in contrast to the processing found in fear, which is considered "bottom-up." With fear, the lower or primitive areas dictate the responses. The immediate danger drives this response. Fear uses simple and well-established pathways that have persisted throughout evolution and do not require thinking to be evoked.

Each type of processing has its own advantages. Anticipatory anxiety is state defined by preparation for danger. Top-down processing allows us to utilize the sophisticated brain areas that make us human, whereas the bottom-up processing of fear allows us to respond immediately, without contemplation. (see Table 3.1)

Table 3.1: Fear Compared to Anticipatory Anxiety

Fear	Anticipatory Anxiety
Evoked by Immediate Danger	Evoked by Future Danger
Instantaneous Reaction	Reaction Waxes and Wanes Over Time
Governed by Primitive Brain Areas	Governed by Higher Brain Areas
Independent of Learning – Hard Wired	Influenced by Learning and Experiences
Expression Universal Among Humans	Expression Dependent on the Individual

The distinctions of the primal-based fear and the human-based anticipatory anxiety may seem academic. After all, who cares what the mechanism is if one is feeling nervous, worried, panicked, anxious, fearful, dreadful, or just stressed out. This concern is understandable, but the most important aspect of mental stress in boxing is that it is yours. Your brain is yours alone, and ownership permits the right to understand how experiences affect how you feel. Examination of mental stress with knowledge allows you to judge how you feel, think, and act. With this examination, the negativity of this mental stress can be used to strengthen your brain and body.

Part II
TRANSFORMING MENTAL STRESS TO STRENGTH: BOXING SMART

THE MENTAL STRESS OF boxing, both anticipatory anxiety and fear, are time-dependent states. Anticipatory anxiety is evoked to prepare for the bout and fear evoked at the bout. However, the danger of fear can be imagined by the brain as immediate, even though it might be weeks away. As such, progression of anticipatory anxiety to fear is not simply a gradual, linear progression. There will be periods of time where you will be stricken with fear well before the bout, when it is not needed. This is normal. However, overall, the mental stress of boxing is characterized by an increase in anticipatory anxiety and then a transition to fear.

As the course of this mental stress is a function of time, how best to use it to your advantage can be broken down with a timeline. How amateur boxing transforms mental stress to strength is presented following a timeline. What timeline to use is somewhat arbitrary. The timeline is going to vary for each individual boxer. However, all boxers should expend the same mental effort. The goal following this timeline is the development of mental strength. In amateur boxing, the development of mental strength is demonstrated by the ability to "box smart."

Boxing smart, as its name implies, is the intelligence needed to box well. The successful boxer has to constantly move his feet, hands, and head in an intelligent manner. The objective of boxing is to punch your opponent while not being punched by him. This is why "stick and move" is the motto of boxing, instead of, perhaps, "hit harder." It is more effective to box smarter than box stronger.

The intelligence, or smarts, needed in boxing is different than the one developed with traditional academics and book learning. With the latter, reasoning and contemplation are fostered. These are the skills needed to progress in academics. With boxing, there is no time for much reasoning or contemplation. The time required for such thinking makes it moot. The sport is too fast and the consequences too severe, to delay action needed pondering your next move. Nonetheless intelligence is required, as the boxer needs to mentally dictate his actions to best prevail.

The focus and concentration needed to box smart is intense. You have an opponent in front of you. You cannot be distracted or divert your mental efforts from your work in the ring and your opponent. This diversion of mental effort is observed physically with the stiffness and predictability of the novice boxer. The novice boxer has yet to learn to box smart. The experienced boxer is not hampered by this impairment. His movements are smooth and coordinated. He is boxing smart.

PART II: TRANSFORMING MENTAL STRESS TO STRENGTH: BOXING SMART

The experienced boxer is boxing smart because he has learned to do so. This type of learning is similar to academic endeavors. The amount of time and effort expended is related to gains achieved. The curriculum, in general terms, can be broken down into three components: boxing skills, boxing strategy, and ring craft.

FOUR

SIX WEEKS OUT: BOXING SKILLS

BOXING SKILLS ARE THE technical movements needed to box. The basic skills are not that complicated. There is the boxer's stance, which is the position you punch out of and defend yourself. There are only four basic types of punches in boxing—the jab, the cross, the uppercut, and the hook. (see Figure 4.1) Defense is to prevent an opponent's punch from scoring and incorporates techniques to evade, deflect, or block an opponent's punch.

However, the number of individual boxing skills is much more than a summation of basic boxing skills. The skills have to be learned in accordance with the anticipated movement of the opponent. That is, how to evade a punch depends on what punch is thrown, the distance between the boxers, and the position of each boxer. Additionally, while there are only four basic punches and a stance, there are many variations of each. Boxing out of an upright stance versus a crouch and countering with a check

Figure 4.1: The Four Basic Types of Punches

hook versus a cross parry are examples of these variations. I am not sure what the grand tally of individual boxing skills is, but it easily runs into the thousands. There are books that provide these techniques, but most boxers learn these techniques in a gym with instruction. Similar to the book learning found in school, one learns the basics and then progress with advanced boxing skills. Also, as in school, the recognition of achievement of these skills requires testing, which in boxing means an opponent and an upcoming bout.

SIX WEEKS OUT: BOXING SKILLS

Arranging the Bout

Danger and the associated mental stress do not emerge until the boxer has a bout scheduled. One competes in sanctioned amateur boxing in two ways. One, a bout is arranged at a single day event, also referred to as a show or card. These bouts are almost always prematched. The opponents are prearranged based on experience, age, and weight. Two, a boxer enters a tournament. Here, the initial bout might be prematched, but the subsequent bouts are determined by progression through the tournament. Amateur boxing tournaments typically occur over days, usually, with one bout per day.

While bouts might be prematched, there is much more of a chance that your opponent will be someone other than the one initially selected. You or your opponent might not make the weight limit, suffer an injury during training, arrive late so another boxer has filled in, or a conflict arises which means that one of you has to pull out, etc. This is not uncommon in amateur boxing, and the preparation reflects this. Amateur boxing preparation is much more focused on developing your strengths rather than preparing for a specific opponent. The preparation in professional boxing is different. Money offers stability to the matchmaking. Preparation focuses a good deal on developing a plan to defeat a specific opponent.

Since your opponent is probably a stranger and may not even be the person you box, the mental stress once the bout is arranged is diffuse and relatively minor. In my case, it does not register in my head that I really have a bout coming up until about six weeks before the show or tournament. At this point, mild anxiety arises and is a reminder that I need to go to the gym on a regular basis and train correctly.

Physical Aspects in Brief

Boxing is a physically strenuous activity and is also efficient exercise. For example, more energy is expended in a boxing training session compared to other exercises such as running on a treadmill. The anticipatory anxiety evoked now is motivation and can be relieved by following the physical exercises offered at the boxing gym. Also, six weeks is a reasonable amount of time to get in the physical shape to box three rounds in an amateur bout.

While boxing workouts vary, there are three basic components. 1) Cardiovascular exercise to promote physical endurance. Distance running, swimming, and cycling are used, with running being the most traditional. 2) Floor exercises such as sit-ups, squats, push-ups, jumping rope, etc., to develop core strength and coordination. 3) High intensity interval training ranging in minutes combined with a shorter interval of rest. This exercise mimics the physical activity in competition. Running sprints, bag work, and sparring are all practiced in this timed manner.

The details of this diverse exercise regimen are outside the scope of the book, but there are a multitude of books that outline various programs. Also, boxing gyms will offer physical exercise programs that can be followed with instruction, all of which promote symmetrical physical development and endurance. Symmetry is required. You have to maintain balance and position to score effectively on your opponent and defend yourself against your opponent's attack.

Boxing has been compared to dancing. Both boxing and dancing require motor precision and coordination in upper and lower limbs to perform a multitude of maneuvers. Both also require anaerobic power to act quickly and vigorously for spurts, as well as aerobic fitness for stamina. Moreover, boxing training, minus sparring, is probably as safe as dancing. The proportional development of the body does not place excessive stress on any one joint. For example, boxers do not suffer noncontact anterior cruciate ligament (ACL) injuries of their knees found in other sports such as basketball.

What boxers do acquire is the characteristic proportioned body with well-developed muscle mass and low body fat. These physical benefits are not just aesthetic, as the anatomy is developed in conjunction with cardiovascular fitness. These physical exercises will provide gains in strength, coordination, balance, and endurance that are a necessity to box. However, utilizing these benefits most effectively requires mental effort and preparation to box smart.

Boxing Skills: Unconscious Activity

The first step in learning to box smart is to acquire boxing skills and then make these skills automatic. From a neuroscience standpoint, this means transitioning these skills from a conscious activity to an unconscious activity. This requires two processes. One, the skill is consciously learned. This is termed "activity-dependent" learning and this is a result of the plasticity of the brain. External influences, the teaching, change neuronal activity in the brain so that there is more neuronal activity, more wiring and power so to speak, devoted to the skill. With repetition, the neuronal connections are fortified and the skill is mastered.

Two, the skill becomes ingrained and stored in the brain, in other words, a memory. Neuroscientists use a number of different terms to describe and classify memory, such as "short-term," "long-term," "working," "associative," "declarative," "procedural," "episodic," "semantic," "explicit," and "implicit", which is reflective of the complexity of the concept. For the neuroscientist, memory is a complex concept as we do not remember everything, nor do we have complete conscious control over the retrieval of memories, and where the memory is formed or stored can be in many areas of the brain. As such, memory may be better and more accurately conceptualized as a process instead of a place.

To master a boxing skill so that it can be performed unconsciously, it needs to be memorized. At the neuronal level, this requires concentrated and long-lasting stimulation. This process has been demonstrated by American psychiatrist Eric Kandel (1929–) who was awarded the Nobel Prize in Medicine and Physiology in 2000 for demonstrating the molecular mechanism of long-term memory in the sea snail *Aplysia*. His observations have been extended to other animal models and have led to a better understanding how the human brain transforms information so that it is memorized.

Memorization of a boxing skill to the point of becoming an unconscious activity, similar as it is found at the neuronal level, requires further repetition and concentration. (see Figure 4.2)

For example, learning to slip a punch is a boxing skill that needs to be automatic for the amateur boxer to box smart. Slipping a punch is a defensive maneuver to avoid an opponent's punch to the head while keeping the boxer within punching range. Physically, slipping is not a physically demanding or complicated maneuver. The boxer shifts and rotates his body slightly, which then moves the head so the punch harmlessly "slips" by. With instruction, one can probably learn the physicality of slipping a punch within five minutes. However, to perform a slip such that it becomes an unconscious activity takes weeks, even months, or years.

Why a very simple activity takes such a long time to become an unconscious activity is the process itself. Much time and mental effort are needed for the boxer to place the conscious activity of

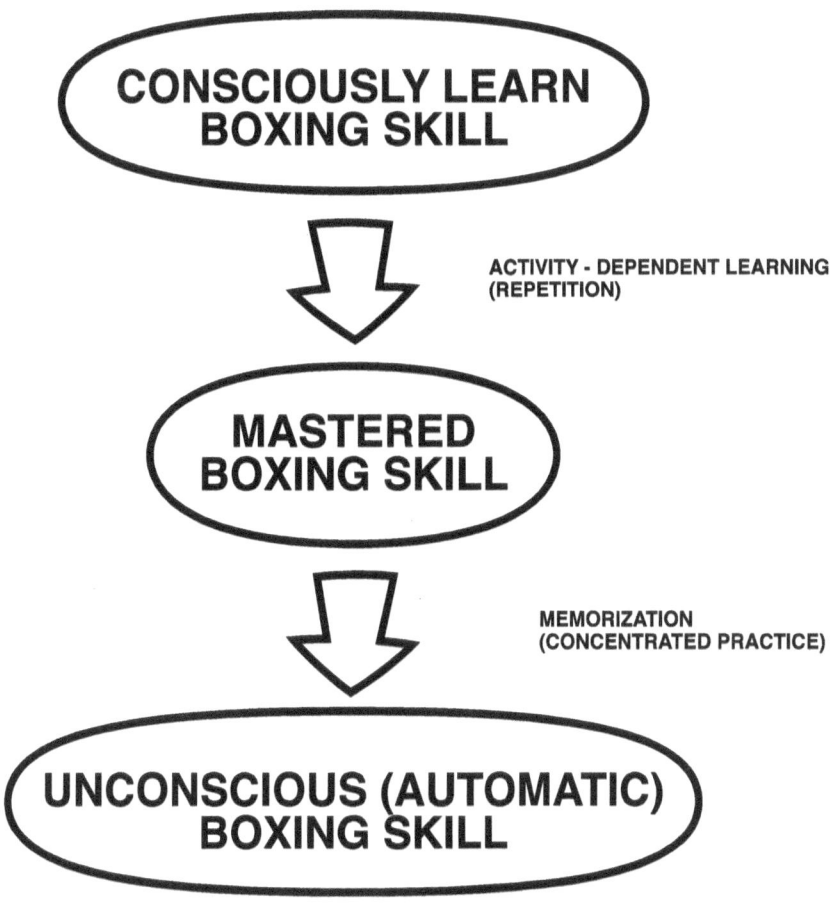

Figure 4.2: Schematic of Transitioning Boxing Skills to the Unconscious

slipping a punch to the unconscious. There are a number of exercises to promote this transformation, one of them being a "slip" bag. A slip bag is small bag, typically six inches or so that is filled with sand or some other heavy material that is suspended by a rope from the ceiling and typically can be adjusted to the head level of the boxer. The boxer pushes the bag so that is oscillates, and then slips the bag as it swings toward his head. (see Figure 4.3) This is a mental exercise, and not much of a physical one. Success requires much more mental concentration than physical endurance. In short, it is a workout primarily for the boxer's brain.

Figure 4.3: Slipping a Punch with the Slip Bag

SIX WEEKS OUT: BOXING SKILLS

Working the slip bag is simple, not physically taxing, but imperative if the boxer is to make the slip an effective tool and part of his repertoire to box smart. Also, unlike the easily quantifiable improvement seen with physical exercise, such as the ability to run farther without fatigue, the improvement in making the slip an unconscious activity is not easily measured while it is being developed. The transformation to the unconscious and the realization of this accomplishment comes when it is needed, that is during sparring or competition.

When the novice boxer first spars, he will slip punches. It takes conscious effort to focus on the opponent to recognize when and where his punches are arriving. Also, conscious effort is expended to follow one of the many axioms of boxing, which in the matter of the slip is to "always hit off the slip." Hitting off the slip is punching immediately after the opponent's punch has been slipped. This is an advantage to exploit at this time. The opponent's guard is down with the punch being thrown and there is no need to move into punching range. The slipping boxer is already there. Slipping and then hitting off the slip is one of the basic maneuvers learned in boxing and becomes progressively easier as one trains.

However, there will be a time in sparring or competition when this maneuver is disrupted. Whether it takes weeks, months, or years from the first time entering the ring, the boxer will slip a punch without thinking to do so. He will move his head out of the way before the thought has entered his brain. The realization of this is jarring, because this is a new experience. It feels as if you have played a magic trick on yourself. Consciously, one questions, did I just do that? Unfortunately, this conscious realization distracts the boxer from the expected follow-through, namely, hitting off the slip. Instead, the boxer's movements freeze as his brain is occupied with what just happened.

Fortunately, this disruption is only temporary. With time and concentrated practice, unconscious activities become more familiar to the boxer's consciousness and are appreciated. With unconscious activity, the boxer reacts quicker, and defensive and offensive maneuvers are performed with precision. In other words, it becomes a habit.

The development of automatic boxing skills does not begin at six weeks out; it starts from the beginning and continues throughout boxing training. Top-notch boxers spend hours on this development even when they have much in their current armament. Like the novice, the boxing skills are memorized by concentrated repetition that begins with slow and measured movements. This ability is forged by many hours at the gym.

Interestingly, the measured and controlled training that boxers actually perform contrasts to how it is typically presented or sold to those outside the gym. For example, training montages are a staple for the promotion of professional boxing. Invariably, these montages show a boxer in a blur of movement punching various boxing bags with an intensity that captivates the viewer. Never mind the voice-over during the montage. The impression on the viewer is that the fury dispensed on those bags will soon be released in the ring.

I enjoy watching these types of productions. They still evoke the same excitement even after many years of seeing the same thing. However, it has limited connection to the reality of training. The only boxers I have seen training like that are beginner boxers who attack a boxing bag with a spasmodic violence that betrays their inexperience. Elite boxers do the opposite. When I was at the gym in medical school, during my entire workout, which was about ninety minutes in its entirety, a professional boxer spent this time punching a piece of tape on a bag. For at least ninety minutes, he would hit that piece of tape. Sometimes he hit it soft, sometimes hard. He would punch the tape from afar and close up, from various angles using different combinations. Three minutes at a time, with a thirty-second respite, that piece of tape took a beating. The beating, however, was not furious, but rather methodical—a function of the concentrated mental effort to do it correctly. He was expending this much mental energy now, so he would not have to think about it in the ring.

So, somewhat paradoxically, to be able to first learn to box smart, you need to practice to the point where you stop thinking. Thinking about boxing skills will slow you down. To avoid being slow, you need to practice in a slow, deliberate manner. You need to slowly travel down a road paved with concentration and instruction.

To make an analogy, this is the same type of instruction given to beginning drivers. Like memorized boxing skills, driving is an example of an unconscious activity. An experienced driver does not have to think of how to work the controls and maneuver the vehicle. The driver's actions are automatic and unconscious. Also, similar to driving, the experienced boxer will develop skills so he does not have to think as much about using them as when he first started.

Transitioning boxing skills from conscious activity to the unconscious activity is essential mental effort. You cannot box smart without this mental investment. This investment is rewarded over time. You will collect a variety of boxing skills that can be summoned automatically. Now, to box smart, you need to learn how to use these skills effectively.

Five
THREE WEEKS OUT: BOXING STRATEGY AND RING CRAFT

THREE WEEKS BEFORE YOUR scheduled bout, the anticipatory anxiety is more intrusive and not as mild. The danger is not as diffuse or abstract as it was just three weeks earlier. Soon, you will be in the ring. While gym exercise programs supply you with boxing skills, no piece of boxing equipment or exercise is going move about the ring or punch like your opponent will soon do. To face an opponent, you need to develop some degree of boxing strategy and ring craft. These are boxing abilities that cannot be developed with gym equipment alone. To be best prepared and properly alleviate mental stress now, you need to spar.

Sparring

Sparring is boxing with an opponent where the aim is not to win, but to educate one or both boxers. The first lesson learned in sparring is to be safe. You both need to avoid injury. You need a healthy sparring partner for effective work. From a practical standpoint, you cannot spar by yourself. If you do not have a sparring partner, you will not get better. Also, at the amateur level, the apprenticeship model for learning is followed, and sparring is usually between boxers of different abilities.

If the novice gets it in his brain that this is an opportune time to prove to himself or the spectators in the gym that he is Rocky Balboa and starts punching as seen in the movies, his experienced sparring partner will "keep it honest." This means that the punishment the novice believes he is dishing out will soon come back at him, promptly delivered by his more experienced opponent. I can attest, as a recipient of this education, this is a lesson quickly learned.

Other than this lesson, you cannot learn if your brain is too occupied with thoughts of being pummeled. As such, the violence is muted. Large gloves are used for safety. Also, while the hands should be wrapped to prevent injury to the hand itself, experienced sparring partners will punch with unclenched fists. This lessens the power of the punch, which is especially important when practicing speed. Faster punches are more powerful than slower ones. Most importantly, at least for novice boxers, the sparring should be supervised by a boxing coach or an experienced boxer.

When first sparring, you will be exhausted within minutes. The mental stress of the situation causes muscle tension. You have yet to learn how to use this tension to your advantage, so it hurts you now by causing more fatigue than it should. Also, your breathing will be disrupted. It takes some time to learn to breathe with a mouthpiece. When first sparring, it is common to bite down on the mouthpiece to such a degree that you will end up holding your breath. Mentally, the fatigue is overwhelming and the urge to quit is predominant. This is normal. Hence the second lesson learned in sparring is not to quit, but to "box to the bell." This is a lesson learned in a stepwise fashion with interval training. Initially, the sparring sessions are of a short duration, maybe a minute per round for the novice.

The encouragement to continue until the timed break not only comes from the instructor outside the ring, but also the sparring partner. If the sparring partner is able to continue, then you should too. With repetition, and the realization that you can make it to the end of a round without passing out, the length of the rounds is gradually increased and rounds of sparring are added.

Not much boxing knowledge is gained in these initial stages. Your brain is focused on basic boxing skills, breathing, and having the energy to box to the end of each round. With time in the ring, these concerns will pass. You then begin to develop your own boxing style.

Boxing Style

With time, effort, and instruction, you will develop a method of boxing that best fits your inherent and practiced advantages. Eventually, a repertoire of your most proficient boxing skills becomes apparent. This collection of boxing skills is referred to as your "boxing style." For example, you may box better pressing the attack. This is referred to as a "pressure" boxing style. Conversely, you may have more ability to counter an attack. You wait for your opponent to make a mistake, and then attack. In doing so, you are using a "counter-puncher" style. There are other general and interesting terms to describe different styles of boxing, such as "jabber," "southpaw," "in-fighter," and so on, but each boxer will have his own style that is usually a variation of the general categories. Your boxing style evolves into what is most comfortable for you.

Boxing Strategy

Boxing strategy is a plan of action to address different types of boxers and boxing styles. This is the forethought of boxing smart. Boxing strategies address various presentations of your opponent. These strategies, being generalized recommendations, are straightforward. For example, boxing strategy against a taller opponent provides useful recommendations to nullify his height advantage. A taller opponent will have leverage and power in punching down. Also, the taller opponent may have longer arms. His reach allows him to punch you from a distance where you cannot punch him. Boxing strategy for the taller opponent is to expect the long-range punch and slip it, then move close which takes away his leverage and allows you to be in your ideal range to punch. You are now at an advantage. His longer arms are of no benefit to him and his longer body gives you a larger area to apply scoring punches. (see Figure 5.1)

Learning the various boxing strategies is not difficult. As described above for a taller opponent, there are useful, general recommendations for other types of boxers and common boxing styles. These simple recommendations have been developed over the thousands of years that boxing has been a sport. Boxing strategy has been proven over time to be effective, but its effectiveness does not make it easy. The difficulty encountered with boxing strategy is in its implementation.

When I was attending medical school, I was sparring at the Bell Recreation Center in Kansas City, Kansas, home of the Rosedale Boxing Club that was adjacent to University of Kansas Medical

Figure 5.1: Boxing Strategy for a Taller Opponent

Center. Kindly, for my benefit alone, Randie Carver, the 1995 National Golden Gloves Champion at 156 lbs. was my sparring partner. Randie was younger, a little taller and leaner than me, but we were pretty much the same size for sparring purposes. Our coach, George Smith, wanted me to get some work for some amateur shows coming up. Randie volunteered to help me out.

Following boxing strategy, I planned to get in close, place my head on Randie's chest where it could not be easily hit and score with punches to the body. Well, that was the plan. In the ring, I never got close enough to Randie to get my head on his chest.

I could not even bridge the distance to punch him. He would step aside to let me pass, punch me not hard, but with enough force to upset my balance, and go in and out of my punching range so I could not determine where he was or would soon be. From my viewpoint, I could not set eyes on his footwork or feints that were leading me one way while he was going another. I could only see that Randie was in front of me. Also, Randie seemed close enough to punch and was punching me, but I could not hit him. After the first round, Randie, with a smile on his face told me, "Nate, I'll stop hitting you in the head if you stop leading with it. Start doubling and tripling up the jab, and have some patience."

The instruction Randie provided is born of experience. Boxing strategy requires experience and further instruction to carry it out. Also, the time-honored boxing strategies do not take into account all of the variables you will encounter. For example, the distance between the boxers is constantly changing. You have to judge not only where your opponent is, but also where he might be going. Then, depending on this distance, you have to decide on the correct punch for that distance. The question is, do you punch where the opponent is or where he might be? This depends on your timing. In fractions of a second, you must determine if you are at the correct distance, with the correct punch, so that it scores where your opponent is or might be.

Change is a given in the boxing ring. The movements and distance between the boxers are constantly changing. The only certainty offered by change is uncertainty. The decision-making in this uncertain milieu, whether to punch or not, etc., also takes place in the midst of violence, where you are punished for contemplation. The boxing ring is not the forum for deliberation, but it is a place where split-second decisions following good judgment are essential.

THREE WEEKS OUT: BOXING STRATEGY AND RING CRAFT

Implementing Boxing Strategy: Intuitive Thinking

Intuitive thinking, also known as intuition or instinct, is an immediate understanding of a situation that is the basis for a decision. The neuroscience of intuitive thinking is considered primarily a subjective, unconscious phenomenon that occurs without the need for objective, conscious reasoning. Also, being a subjective experience, that is, an experience based on you yourself, does not mean it only relies on you. The effectiveness of intuitive thinking is directly related to the instruction you receive while sparring. You are given guidance about what you should do to the point it becomes intuitive. Eventually, unconsciously, you will recognize a situation and immediately react.

Intuitive thinking is related to experience and is honed during sparring. While you are sparring, the instructor will point out vulnerabilities of your opponent where sound strategy will give you an advantage. These vulnerabilities will not be apparent to you at first. Hence the need for overt guidance. For example, in the course of sparring you may not detect that your opponent is dropping his right hand from his guard position. This makes your opponent vulnerable to a left hook. The instructor will urge you to start throwing left hooks. You then maneuver yourself to a position and punch in combinations that are favorable to throwing left hooks. Obviously, your opponent can hear this too, so the first one thrown most likely will be ineffective, as your opponent's vulnerability is no longer there, that is, his guard is back up, he has moved out of range, he is now punching you, etc. However, with time in the ring and the correct guidance, you become accustomed to reacting to your opponent dropping his right hand. This situation becomes familiar, and the reaction of throwing left hooks becomes intuitive.

The reinforcement or reward for intuitive thinking is insight. Insight is the conscious awareness of a solution. When boxing smart with effective boxing strategy you are rewarded with conscious thoughts of success. Your instincts have led to the correct solution. (see Figure 5.2)

This conscious reinforcement is needed. It is support for continuing with strategies and skills that are effective now. It is also reinforcement for the high degree of concentration needed for the remainder of the bout. While intuitive thinking is primarily unconscious, it requires an accurate perception of the situation. You have to keep your eyes open and focus on your opponent, so your brain can correctly register and react to a constantly changing and

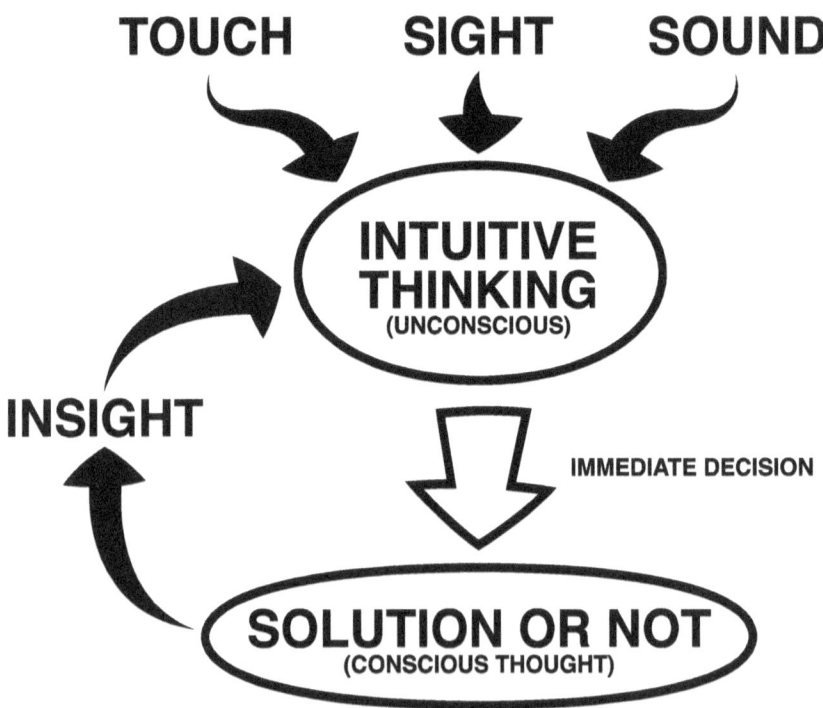

Figure 5.2: Schematic of Intuitive Thinking and Insight

violent environment. Distraction disrupts this process, impairing your instincts, and this is no way to box smart.

When you follow your instincts, you free up mental activity for more sophisticated boxing strategies. For example, "setting up punches," is an advanced strategy where you create vulnerabilities in your opponent. This is not just reacting, but dictating a situation where you will be most effective. A simple example of this is throwing a punch at your opponent's shoulder. This punch is not a scoring punch, but is landed to better determine distance, disrupt your opponent's balance, or make him move so he is more vulnerable to the following punch.

Implementing boxing strategy is an achievement. Demonstrating these sophisticated boxing abilities, obviously, will take more than three weeks to master. Nonetheless, the anticipatory anxiety generated for the upcoming bout is alleviated with this worthwhile effort. However, the smart boxer knows this is not enough. Sometimes boxing strategy fails.

Ring Craft

Mike Tyson (1966–) famously said, "Everyone has a plan until they get punched in the face." It is hard to argue with Mike. You will only find out if your plan is effective when you box. The boxing strategy that you and your seconds have brought to the bout may not work. Despite your thorough preparation, there will be times when your boxing strategy is ineffective for this specific opponent. During these times, insight is provided by your opponent's punches rather than your own. Getting punched in the face repeatedly is a clear indication that your boxing strategy is a failure. You need to change your plan. You need boxing strategy that provides a solution to defeat this opponent. You now turn to ring craft.

The ability to solve boxing problems as they present in the ring is termed "ring craft." In other words, ring craft is your ability to use the correct boxing strategy to better your opponent. You have to solve the individual problem that is your opponent. Ring craft is what you rely on when you need a solution during the bout.

Methodology of Ring Craft

When you are being punched in the face, you will be frustrated. You will question your boxing strategy and may be at a loss about what to do. You will also be embarrassed. This assault is occurring while people are watching. The frustration and embarrassment will impair your concentration, and you need to focus on your opponent. Every boxing match has ebbs and flows. There will be times when you can better apply your current boxing strategy or change your boxing strategy to your advantage.

To utilize ring craft, you have to stay in the moment. Only by staying in the moment will you be able to sense and seize advantages when they arise. Your solution will come to you when you are fully aware and not distracted by frustration and embarrassment. Ring craft also requires for you to be calm. When you are calm, you can think with clarity. You need this clarity. You now have to outsmart your opponent who has a better plan than you.

You also need calmness and clarity to successfully receive and implement advice. The respite between rounds is not only for physical recuperation. This respite allows consultation with your seconds. They are in your corner to give you guidance on your boxing strategy. Being outside the ring, they will offer you a different perspective; a perspective that may not be apparent while in the midst of the bout. This may be key information that you now can use to defeat your opponent.

When you successfully employ ring craft, repeatedly being punched in the face is behind you. Ring craft has provided you boxing strategy that works. You start to control the action in the ring. You punch when the opportunity arises and move to the correct space at the right time to avoid being punched. You box as you should and want to, which is what your opponent does not want you to do. You are boxing smart.

The Art of Ring Craft

Ring craft is the apex of boxing smart. Though compared to the two other components of boxing smart, this type of intelligence requires the study of art rather than science.

Looking back at boxing skills and strategy, science is the cornerstone for their development. They are techniques obtained and advanced with science. Boxing skills are reduced to their essential movements and mastered. Boxing strategy is a plan to best use these skills. There are many books that define boxing skills and strategy. These are similar to textbooks used to learn science-based information in other fields, such as medicine.

Ring craft, though, is more than technical skill and strategy. Ring craft is the application of these abilities, and this application cannot be reduced to a specific technique. Ring craft transcends technique. As such, ring craft cannot be presented or learned with words alone. There are no books that will fully define and teach you ring craft. I could write hundreds of pages on particular boxing skills and strategies to best demonstrate ring craft, but all of those words would be wrong. There are too many variables.

It is impossible for me to write about what is best for you against a boxer who may or may not do what I write about him doing.

While you cannot study ring craft reading a book, the intelligence needed for ring craft is provided in a manner that is similar to a physician's education. This is demonstrated by the work both fields use to develop the required intelligence. When first learning medicine, education is initially provided by instruction with textbooks. This is the science of medicine, and is similar to the boxer first learning boxing skills and strategy. Like boxing, medical education and training follows the apprenticeship model. Medical students and resident physicians learn to care for patients under the guidance and supervision of attending physicians. These are the sparring sessions for learning physicians.

After years of preparation, the physician completes his training. He is now a practitioner. Like the boxer in competition, his decisions are his own. The health of his patients will depend on his diagnostic acumen and recommended treatment. In other words, his skill and strategy, and this will soon be challenged. A patient will present with distress that does not match pathology of prior patients or what is presented in medical textbooks. This patient's symptoms do not synchronize with a syndrome and the course of illness is characterized by its lack of resemblance to what he has observed before. This patient is a diagnostic conundrum.

This patient presentation is referred to as a "challenging case," and is a normal part of medical practice. The medical thinking and intelligence needed to successfully care for this patient are the same smarts the boxer with ring craft employs. Both concentrate and focus on the person. The problem requires further evaluation. The boxer notices a trend of his opponent punching with a right-handed cross after immediately leading with a left jab. This is referred to as a "1–2 combination." If this trend continues, the boxer can exploit it to his advantage because it is now predictable. The physician listens to his patient carefully. Each patient has his own perspectives shaped by his heredity and experience. Disease will also manifest through this patient's perspective. This stoic patient may provide a different account of the same disease than an ebullient one. The boxer and the physician are getting to know this person.

If this examination does not provide a solution, the boxer and physician also have the intelligence to seek consultation; the boxer with his seconds between rounds, the physician with his colleagues. New perspectives are provided with consultation. The boxer and physician now have new ideas, and a different course of action may be taken. Patience is also needed. This challenging opponent or patient requires time for the solution to become apparent.

This type of thinking provides the boxer and physician additional knowledge to better understand his opponent or patient. This is the intelligence needed to find solutions when there are none to be found in a book. Solutions arise when this opponent and patient are addressed as individuals. With this added perspective and input, he identifies aspects that are particular to this individual and make him unique. The uniqueness of this opponent or patient, what makes him him, is now known. He is no longer a puzzle or a problem. This is practicing the art of ring craft or the art of medicine.

Ring craft is an art, which is only developed by experience as a practitioner. There is no other study. As you gain experience with opponents, you will develop solutions for a variety of different opponents. With these experiences, you will strengthen your ring craft. Moreover, acquiring ring craft is a lifetime pursuit that is never really completed. Each time you step out of the ring, you will have learned. This learning never stops.

While you will never completely master ring craft, its attainment is your goal. Learning to box smart is the correct preparation for your upcoming bout. But there is one more barrier to pass before you face your opponent. You are going have to win the bout with yourself.

Six
TWO DAYS OUT: YOU VERSUS YOU

Psychobabble

THE SKEPTICAL READER MIGHT think that "you versus you" is expected psychobabble from a psychiatrist writing a book on boxing. By definition, boxing requires a fellow combatant. Additionally, in amateur boxing, where there are rarely draws, you versus you seems absurd. There are simply winners and losers in amateur boxing. How can you defeat or lose to yourself? And why should you spend effort on doing so?

Whether this is psychobabble or not, you versus you is a paradox. There is no denying that, but every boxer who competes will have this struggle. This is a boxing truth. It is the same type of truth that we all encounter in life. These are truths with academic validation. In the humanities, one can appreciate a love that hurts. In physics, one can appreciate that an electron behaves as a particle or wave. Paradoxes abound and do not escape the human condition. And, while a boxing ring is small, it can fit in quite a bit of the human condition.

Being two days out from your bout means that your preparation is completed. Whatever physical and mental shape you have developed is not going to be improved with more training at this stage. In fact, more physical training at this stage is a detriment. Your body needs some rest to recover from the hard training you have put in. Considering this, your brain should be at ease.

No. The honest reality of being two days out from your bout is that your brain is fraught with unease. This is normal. Any boxer who says he is never worried, scared, frightened, nervous, etc., a couple of days before a bout is a liar. The experienced boxer knows this is normal and has figured out how to alleviate this distress. You may be overwhelmed, questioning, "Is this a good idea?" "Maybe there is something to be said for peace, love, and understanding. Why fight?" No worries. These thoughts cannot defeat the fact that you are a born fighter. We all are. At this stage, you have to understand your brain is your opponent. There is no denying this. Neither is there any mystery why this is the case. During the weeks of thoughtful preparation, anticipatory anxiety is a good motivation to box smart. The mental and physical symptoms of anticipatory anxiety are alleviated. However, the purpose of anticipatory anxiety is not only to prepare for danger, but also to avoid it.

Rationally, the upcoming bout is safe. While you may clearly understand that you will be safe and the danger is not as bad as one would think, this does not register with your brain. Mother Nature—that is, anticipatory anxiety—overrides reason. The symptoms of anticipatory anxiety are significantly and unconsciously increased as it attempts to serve its function and avoid danger. Again, this is normal. Naturally, one will have feelings of doubt and dread. Physically, one will be tense. Also, insomnia, the lack of sleep, will set in. Insomnia is ubiquitous at this stage for the novice boxer. It is one of the battles of you versus you where the outcome is easily determined. You sleep before your bout or you do not.

Sleep

All living in the animal kingdom have a rest-activity cycle. The need for rest is essential for life. If it is prevented in animals, as shown experimentally, life is drastically shortened. This rest in humans is sleep and the need to sleep is unavoidable. This is unlike eating, for example, where an individual can starve himself to the point of death.

Human sleep has been categorized into two distinct states: rapid eye movement (REM) and non-rapid eye movement (NREM). The flow between the two states during sleep is defined by the electrical pattern of the brain as recorded by electroencephalography (EEG). NREM sleep is the first type of sleep during the cycle and generally is characterized by a slowing of the body. NREM sleep is divided into four stages. Stage 1 sleep is the transitional stage between wakefulness and sleep that lasts about five minutes. Stage 2 sleep lasts for approximately forty to sixty minutes. It is preparation for the deep sleep of the next two stages. Stages 3 and 4 sleep have similar EEG patterns and are referred to as deep sleep. Deep sleep lasts for about twenty to thirty minutes. Entering deep sleep is important because these stages are required to reduce the need for sleep. (see Figure 6.1)

REM sleep is the last stage of the cycle and typically lasts for twenty minutes. The EEG pattern during REM sleep resembles the waking state. Physically, the limb muscles become temporarily

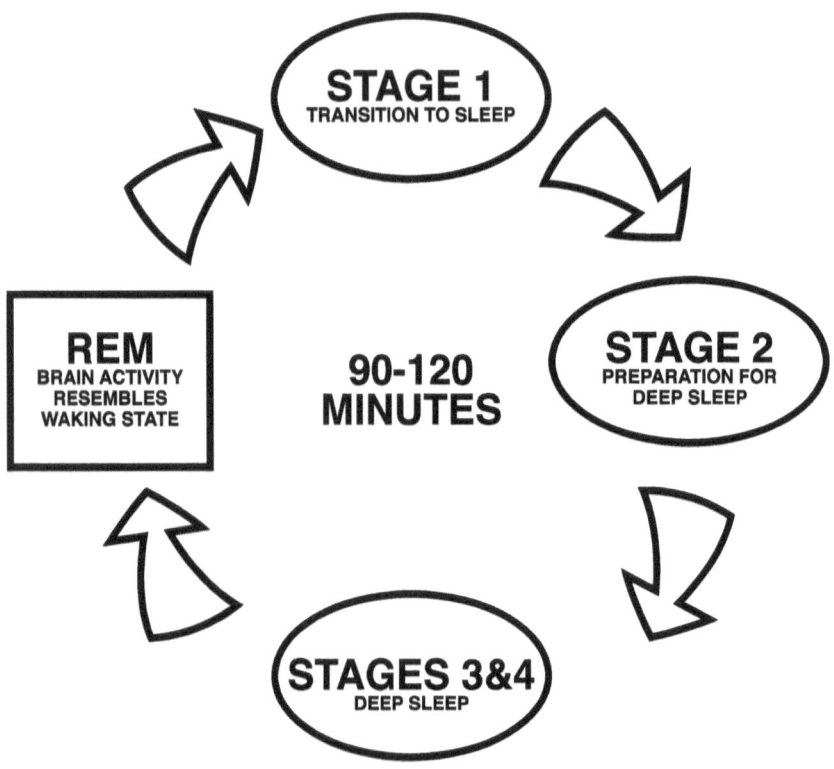

Figure 6.1: Stages of Sleep

paralyzed, blood pressure rises, breathing becomes labored and the eyes move about rapidly. (Hence the name rapid eye movement.) Psychologically, this is the stage of dreams. Much has been written on the meaning of dreams: Austrian neurologist Sigmund Freud (1856–1939) believed that dreams were a portal into the unconsciousness and Swiss psychiatrist Carl Jung (1875–1961) spent most of his career describing a framework into which the symbols of dreams could be understood. The content of dreams can be analyzed and an individual may gain insight into his life, but from a strictly scientific viewpoint, the "why" of dreams is unknown. What has been repeatedly shown is that REM sleep is needed for new learning. When individuals are deprived of REM sleep, they cannot recall newly learned material.

A typical sleep cycle averages an hour and a half and there are four to six cycles per night in an average night's sleep of eight hours. The sleep cycle is not static and changes as the night progresses. The percent of Stages 3 and 4 sleep is highest in the beginning and decreases throughout the night, while REM periods increase in length throughout the night.

There are two processes in the body that determine when it is time to sleep and they are independent of each other. The first process is called "homeostasis." Homeostasis is the medical term for equilibrium or balance. This is simply that the likelihood of sleep increases as the period of wakefulness increases. No matter how much one may try, if one stays up long enough, sleep will occur. The second is called the circadian (Latin for "about the day") process. This is commonly referred to as the "biological clock." This is a "clock" in the body that is "set" by the light of day and the dark of night. The clock is located in a specific area of the brain called the suprachiasmatic nucleus and it receives input from the retina of the eyes.

Insomnia

Insomnia is the inability to fall asleep or remain sleeping for an adequate length of time. Insomnia is very common because so many mental states and physical conditions can cause insomnia. Mental illness, substance abuse, and a wide variety of medical conditions are some of the underlying culprits. Included within these potential causes of insomnia is anticipatory anxiety.

How anticipatory anxiety affects sleep is generally understood. Anticipatory anxiety increases adrenaline in the brain and body. In the brain, the increase in adrenaline disrupts the transition from arousal to sleep. It also overrides the normal inhibition of arousal that occurs during sleep. In the body, the increased adrenaline causes muscle tension. All of these factors contribute to insomnia.

Anticipatory anxiety and the resultant insomnia is a detriment. You are as prepared as you are going to be. Rest is needed. Fortunately, for the short-term, there are many effective medications that can help initiate and propagate sleep. And, at the same time, some of these medications can also lower anticipatory anxiety. For example, lorazepam, diphenhydramine, chloral hydrate, and quetiapine are different psychotropic medications with different mechanisms of actions. All of these medications can effectively quell insomnia and lower anticipatory anxiety. Of course, this being boxing, none of these medications are appropriate.

While these and similar medications are effective, this effectiveness is a contraindication for you as an amateur boxer. Simply, no matter the mechanism of action for each particular medication, they all exert their therapeutic effect by sedating brain function and, with some medications, muscle function. Also, while the therapeutic effect is ideally the eight hours needed for sleep, the medications are still in the body after exerting their therapeutic effect. These medications can stay in your system for days, even weeks. This is no problem for patients with insomnia, as the therapeutic effect has worn off. However, for you, these medications will still be in the body slowing brain function and possibly muscle function during your bout.

You should not notice this subtherapeutic effect on wakefulness, but the psychotropic medications are still in your body. You will be placed at a disadvantage when entering the ring with such medication. Boxing fitness and performance requires instantaneous decisions and coordination of muscle movements in fractions of a second that are governed primarily by unconscious brain function. Even considering all the mental and physical preparation you have put in for the upcoming bout, your ability will be compromised by these medications.

Psychotropic medications are not an option for your insomnia. You will be awake, and this arousal is fueled by anticipatory anxiety. One of the core components of anticipatory anxiety is negativity. This negativity will manifest in your thoughts. Also, another characteristic of thoughts of anticipatory anxiety-generated insomnia is that they are "ruminations." Ruminations are defined medically and have a slightly different meaning than the lay definition to ruminate, which is to contemplate or deliberate about an idea. In gastroenterology, rumination is the partial digestion and the subsequent regurgitation of food found in some gastrointestinal disorders and normal in cows. In psychiatry, rumination more closely follows the gastroenterology definition in that a rumination is a repetitive, negative thought that persists.

These ruminations will be distressing for you and made worse by the persisting insomnia. This is normal. This is your brain trying to avoid the danger of the upcoming bout. The content will vary among individual boxers, but the character and pattern are universal. Also universal for the boxer is that he can defeat this insomnia. In other words, you are the means.

Mental Strategy for You versus You

One of the appeals of the inherent paradox of you versus you is that you control who the winner is. Also, you are aware that anticipatory anxiety is harmful two days before the bout. As written earlier, anticipatory anxiety is a top-down brain activity that is governed by sophisticated, conscious areas of the brain. Anticipatory anxiety is ruled by conscious thought. With conscious thought, you can quell anticipatory anxiety which will allow you to sleep. You can defeat your insomnia.

The problem with this is that you have to figure out what conscious thoughts are effective. I cannot tell you what to think to defeat your insomnia. I do not know who you are or the content of your negative ruminations before your bout. The negative ruminations of anticipatory anxiety-generated insomnia will be different for each of us. We are all our own person. What is negative in my brain, what I dread, will be different than what you experience. What I do to alleviate this will be different than what you do.

While I cannot tell you what to think, I will give you some strategic direction. First, do what you need to do to win. The right thoughts or strategies are the ones that allow you to sleep. Second, you also need to be honest about what works and what does not. When you enter the ring, you will find it is an honest place, perhaps unsettlingly honest. You cannot fake boxing. In the ring, there is no place to hide and your true abilities will be on display. You need to be honest in your preparation.

What I do to stop the unneeded anticipatory anxiety adheres to these two guidelines. My strategy is on my own terms and it works. It is honest in this way. Perhaps presenting my mental strategy will give you guidance to defeat your insomnia. Your mental strategy will be of your own choosing, with your own rules, and on your own terms. You will discover what is best for you. You will win.

TWO DAYS OUT: YOU VERSUS YOU

Me versus Me

When I was in college and medical school, without the scientific knowledge and experience I have now, I knew that if I stayed up, I would be more tired and ready to sleep the next night. If I had insomnia two nights before my bout, I would stay up by playing solitaire or cribbage if some of my roommates were up. I would make sure not to take a nap the following day. The night before my bout, I would sleep because I was tired.

This was fine in my early twenties, but in middle age, being a professional and with children, I cannot stay up all night playing cards. When I have insomnia a couple of nights before my bout—and I do—I am left to my thoughts. Invariably, I will have thoughts about my opponent, who is usually a stranger. At times, even though I know that my opponent will be around my age, with the same age-centric responsibilities, my brain will ruminate. These thoughts are negative. I imagine I am about to encounter a boxer who is bigger, better, and more prepared than me. While I know this is not true, as mismatches are not part of amateur boxing, such ruminations drain my confidence. This, in itself, is distressing. Not only will I be tired from the insomnia, I will be without confidence, and about to enter the ring with a budding Attila the Hun.

Confidence is a positive emotion that emerges in accordance with one's perception of competence. As a mental state, confidence fluctuates based on my abilities and my perception of them. I know that my bout will be with a boxer of roughly the same competence. I also know that I have trained to box smart. My confidence should be fine, and it is until I have insomnia.

Before the bout, the insomnia grinds away at my confidence while I toss and turn no matter if my thoughts have no validity.

This is a common effect associated with anticipatory anxiety-generated insomnia. The negativity decreases my confidence. There is also a common and effective mental health treatment for this negativity called "cognitive behavioral therapy" (CBT). CBT is the psychological treatment of choice for those with insomnia as a result of anticipatory anxiety.

Addressing the validity of thoughts is one of the bedrocks of CBT. In short, patients who employ CBT question the validity of their thoughts. With this questioning, patients realize that the attendant negative emotions have no basis in logic. For example, I know that my thoughts are not true. My opponent is not an Attila the Hun. He will be a fair match. Moreover, the bout will be safe. I will box well. It is what I have prepared to do and have done before. With repetition, the associated negative emotions evoked by the thoughts are lessened. With CBT you train your brain not to be negative because there is no valid reason to be negative. Without this negativity, the ruminations dissipate and sleep ensues.

Unfortunately and honestly, for me, this technique offers no relief. It should, but it does not. CBT for this is not my solution, though it may be yours. Successful treatment in patients with the same condition varies. Even though the condition is the same and the endpoint is sleep, the solutions are different. This is just the way it is.

Even without CBT, I still have to sleep. I still have to win me versus me. And I do. Simply, I stop fighting. I welcome and endorse the negativity that is supplied by anticipatory anxiety. Valid or not, I let the negativity run over my confidence. I wish I could write that my succumbing to the negativity is noble. I could attribute my welcoming the negativity as dissent. I could label this behavior as a sign of distinction and call myself a contrarian. To be honest, though, I have given in to the opponent in my brain, the Attila the Hun I have imagined.

It is no big deal if I lose. I am in good shape, better than when I started getting ready. This itself is a win. And who cares if I win or lose? Probably no one else other than me, and I am fine with losing. I may stay up for a bit and hum a requiem for my demise, but all in all, I get to sleep comfortably soon after I concede defeat to my upcoming opponent.

This is my go-to method if I cannot sleep and it works. Fighting the negativity is not my solution. I surrender to the negativity, but on my own terms. It successfully alleviates the anticipatory anxiety that is the underlying cause of the insomnia. Again, for your bout, it will be you versus you, and this does not include me. You will have insomnia, as it is a normal function of anticipatory anxiety. Moreover, you may have thoughts that make the upcoming bout seem more difficult than it will be. Fortunately, you can control and alleviate these thoughts with conscious effort. What that effort is depends on what works for you.

Transitioning from Anticipatory Anxiety to Fear

Anticipatory anxiety will continue as the bout approaches, but will eventually run its course until the danger cannot be avoided. This will have some mental and physical effects. These are signs that you are transitioning from you versus you to you versus him, which is, in essence, transitioning from anticipatory anxiety to fear.

Hopefully, after a good night of sleep you awake the day of your bout feeling positive with the rejuvenation that sleep allows. At the weigh-in and medical exam you will meet your opponent or potential opponents. The anticipatory anxiety here is a bit less.

Now you know you have an opponent and your bout is scheduled. The frustration of not having an opponent when you have trained as hard as you have and, most likely, have family and friends carving out time to watch you evokes anxiety itself. Confirmation that you will be actually competing in the ring alleviates these concerns. Also, the process of every amateur boxer undergoing a weigh-in and medical exam is time-consuming and boring. You will be waiting a good amount of time. It is important to pass this time in doing things that will distract you, such as speaking with the other boxers, listening to music, reading, etc. These distractions lower your anticipatory anxiety.

Once this process has been completed, the show card, the schedule of bouts, will soon be posted and then you will know when you will be competing. Typically, this will be hours away, and anticipatory anxiety returns. Now is the time to employ mental maneuvers that will keep you calm. There is no benefit in getting amped-up hours before your bout. Maybe you will find peace of mind by listening to music, meditating, or thinking about your boxing strategy, etc. What I do is leave the facility.

I do not like to be around other boxers who are getting ready. Also, since I like to get my hands wrapped very close to my bout, there is no need to be at the show and have this done hours before. Seeing other boxers prepare and having my hands wrapped hours before my bout infects my brain with adrenaline rushes well before they are needed. These are episodes of fear that are best avoided by simply leaving. I also leave because I like to have something light to eat before I box, and I will need a bathroom soon.

Like the normal and predictable insomnia noted in anticipatory anxiety, an easily quantifiable sign that one is transitioning from anticipatory anxiety to fear is the need to defecate. No matter how regularly you defecate, most of you will defecate before your bout. This is normal and has a clear medical explanation; it is simply a sign that fear is emerging.

There are a number of factors that lead to defecation. The specific physiology is outside the scope of this book and my expertise, but there are some basic tenets that are applicable. Generally, one is more prone to defecation after one eats and less prone to defecation while one sleeps. This is the function of normal regulation of the colon by the brain and nerve reflexes. One component of this regulation is the vagus nerve. The vagus nerve, its name derived from the Latin word for "wandering," is named because it has many connections with multiple organs as it travels from the brain to the intestine. (see Figure 6.2)

The vagus nerve is the longest of the cranial nerves and is involved in many bodily functions. Its primary role is to mediate parasympathetic outflow to a number of organs including the heart, lung, and gastrointestinal tract. Input from the vagus nerve to the colon is primarily an unconscious activity as the vagus nerve is part of the autonomic nervous system. Being regulated by the autonomic nervous system, your unconscious brain primarily controls defecation. As such you cannot defecate on command, that is with volitional conscious thought. You defecate only when your brain and body deem it necessary and practical. For example, it's practical to open up more of the gastrointestinal tract for digestion after eating and not when sleeping.

Fear can impact this regulation, and it is thought to be done by impacting the function of the vagus nerve. The dorsal motor nucleus of the vagus nerve, which is found in the brain stem, is affected by the unconscious sympathetic outflow triggered by fear. The exact mechanism of how fear influences the vagus nerves is debated, but the leading hypothesis is that sympathetic outflow of fear causes an increase in vagus nerve function by the brain

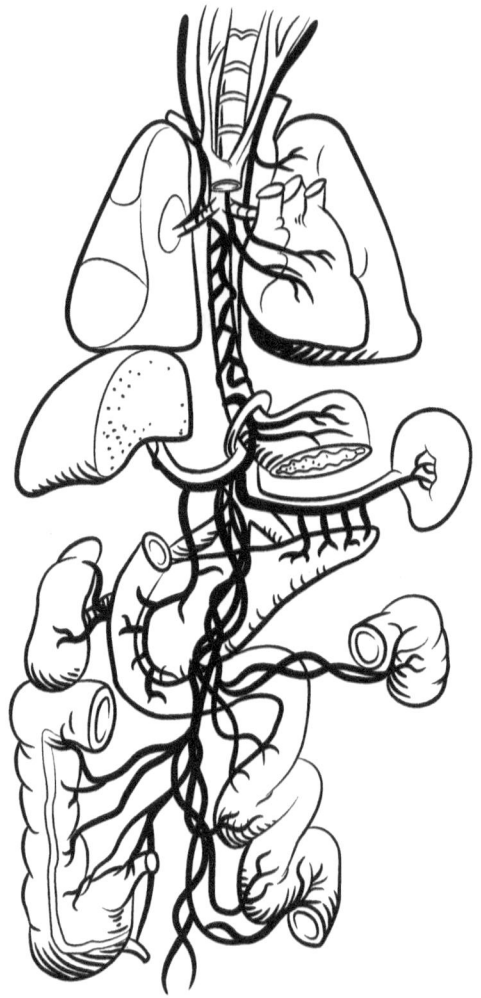

Figure 6.2: The Vagus Nerve

trying to counterbalance the sympathetic outflow of fear with parasympathetic stimulation of the vagus nerve. Whether this is the case or not, the end result is that fear promotes stimulation of the vagus nerve activity in the gastrointestinal tract causing the colon to contract. This contraction leads to defecation.

TWO DAYS OUT: YOU VERSUS YOU

The entire process is independent of conscious thought. It is triggered by fear. Fear is normal now. The bout is unavoidable. I know I will have to defecate sometime before my bout and will consciously make sure I am at a place, a restaurant, or hotel room where I can go to the bathroom in relative peace.

Defecation does not fit into a warrior narrative, but most boxers will admit their need to do this before a bout. Throughout my boxing experience, I have never had pre-bout thoughts of victory inspired by the fighting spirit of sick babies or freedom. Instead, I think I will have to defecate soon. Also, while not as ubiquitous as defecation, fear can also influence the vagus nerve to affect other areas of the gastrointestinal tract. When I was in medical school, I was boxing at an amateur show that was held at a country and western bar in Kansas City. The bathroom of the bar was also the changing room for the amateur boxers in the show. While in this bathroom, there was a person retching in a stall and obviously vomiting. Thinking that this was a patron who had drank too much, I was surprised to see a fellow boxer emerge from the stall. Noticing me and my surprise, he calmly smiled and said, "I'm ready."

SEVEN

THE BOUT: YOU VERSUS HIM

THERE IS NO FINAL bell to signal the end of you versus you, but you will know when this bout is done. You will have the same feeling as the boxer who finished vomiting before his bout, which is a sense of relief. The anticipatory anxiety that you have been experiencing for weeks and with more acuity days before your bout is gone. While you will still have sensations of fear, mentally you have less stress than you felt hours earlier. To make an analogy, it is similar to how one feels riding a roller coaster at an amusement park. The anticipation evoked during the initial ascent is longer and more uncomfortable than the excitement experienced during the descent.

When this occurs will vary for each boxer. For me, the anticipatory anxiety comes to an end when I get my hands wrapped. Regarding hand wraps, you should have your hands wrapped at least thirty minutes before your bout, since the wraps need to be inspected by an official. Also, make sure the wrap is done by someone who has experience. There are specific rules regarding the placement of tape, length of the wrap, type of wrap, etc., and having to have your hands wrapped again because they were placed incorrectly adds unneeded stress.

Once officially approved, consciously, and most likely unconsciously, I know the only way these wraps are coming off my hands is when they are cut off after the bout. This is a relief for me. I now know that my brain needs to be clear to box well, which is boxing smart. This does not mean my brain is clear now, as the anticipatory anxiety has been replaced with fear. I also know that the fear I have now is going to help me if I use it correctly. I need to utilize what fear offers in the ring, and not waste any of its benefits. To do this I need to be calm and have a sense of serenity, which is the gold standard for any boxer who is about to enter the ring.

Serenity

Berserkers were legendary Norse warriors who fought with a fury that was attributable to their lunacy. They reportedly went into battle foaming at the mouth, biting their shields, and in a mental state that made them impervious to pain. Whether berserkers were actual warriors or a legend to create fear in the adversaries of the Vikings, the concept has remained to this day with the word, "berserk," an adjective to describe uncontrollable anger and violence. Berserkers may have had their place on ancient battlefields and given the English language a colorful word, but uncontrollable anger and violence offers no benefit in boxing. Instead, serenity is needed.

Boxing is about control. You need to control the action so you box successfully. In other words, the goal is to do what you want

THE BOUT: YOU VERSUS HIM

to do, not what your opponent wants you to do. To best do this, you need to be calm, the opposite of the berserker. You need to have a serenity that allows you to box smart. And this is reflected in the preparation right before you enter the ring.

How you create and maintain this composure will be up to you, but you will have assistance from your coach. In the thirty minutes or so before your bout, in soft-spoken words, your coach will go over strategy. Maybe both of you have observed your opponent preparing before the bout and noticed a particular boxing style. Perhaps he is warming up as a southpaw. You will now practice maneuvers that might be effective against a southpaw. Whatever the case, this preparation right before the bout should be delivered and executed in a calm manner.

This type of preparation is helpful, but you will also have to call upon mental strategies to keep your serenity. After all, you will soon be in the ring alone with a stranger who is set on punching you. This will naturally evoke fear.

There is no way to avoid fear in the boxing ring. The options for flight are gone, and fear is what we now innately have in order to fight. Fear will help you as it is your body's natural state to fight. Fear is what drives us unconsciously to perform better. Fear keeps our eyes focused on our opponent, supplies oxygen to our working muscles, increases the energy in our efforts, and allows one to react before one can think. Thus, fear allows us to respond quickly and then accurately. Without fear, you would not be able to box as well as you have the potential to do. However, you do not need to have these sensations outside of the ring. This will drain energy from you before it is needed. Fear can also disrupt your serenity. In the minutes before your bout, you have to temper your fear.

Confidence

"Yesterday, I was lying. Today, I'm telling the truth."

— Bob Arum, Esq.
American Professional
Boxing Promoter (1931–)

Mr. Arum attributes his famous quotation to the effects of drinking with a group of sportswriters, but it also can be interpreted as knowing quite a bit about boxing and confidence. Yesterday, I accepted thoughts of losing. I needed to sleep, and this was part of the plan. Today, I want to win. Thankfully, I was able to sleep last night. If I had not, then I would be tired and without the confidence I have here and now.

At this stage, confidence is required. Confidence is a positive emotion. Confidence is not needed to sleep, but is a must when in the ring. Confidence lessens the inherent negativity that emerges with fear. As I have said, confidence is the mental perception of competence. You have to be confident about your abilities, that is, your competence as a boxer.

Confidence will help you win your bout. In fact, confidence is what all athletes develop to prepare for competition. With confidence, the athlete is in a positive mental state. From a mental standpoint, confidence breeds optimism. The competition is not as daunting. The athlete then can focus his mental efforts on positive imagery. He will envision himself performing successfully.

You will latch on to confidence in the moments before your bout. You will use this confidence to work with your seconds on boxing strategy. You will have a plan of action and see yourself in the ring implementing this plan. This positive thinking and imagery are sound preparation for your performance in the ring. You are preparing to box smart.

Confidence also fluctuates. This is normal. Fear will vary in the moments before your bout. You need the correct amount of confidence to counter the negativity of your fear. Having the correct amount of confidence is important. While a positive emotion, the amount needs to be right. Too much or too little confidence is hazardous.

This hazard is encountered when your mental preparation strays from focus on performance to the result. You need confidence to win, but not for the win. The win is a result, not a performance. This is an important distinction. Confidence is needed to prepare you for and during your bout. It is not needed after your bout, when you find out if you have won or lost. You want to win, but winning is a fact that will be determined *after* your bout. With words, this distinction may seem obvious. However, in vivo, the clarity is smudged by fear.

You will be fearful in the moments before your bout. You will or have been trying to bolster your confidence to match your fear. In this state, you may be more apt to focus on the win to increase your confidence. You may be imagining yourself with your hand raised, or accepting the winning trophy or belt, or your victory speech.

With these thoughts, your confidence has risen to hubris. Hubris is what led to Icarus's demise, and you will be more susceptible than him. Unlike Daedalus warning his son to avoid flying too close to the sun, your family and friends will not warn you. They will do the exact opposite. On the day of your bout, you will be told repeatedly that you are going to win. This is what family and friends do at boxing matches. It would be odd if they did not. They have the best intentions. They not only want you to win, but are also trying to increase your confidence so you do win.

Beware of the win. Thoughts of the win will burn you. Mental imagery of you celebrating your win with family and friends or trying out words for your victory speech are not going to help you during your bout. Hubris takes valuable time away from you, time you should be concentrating on boxing strategy.

Too little confidence is another hazard. Without enough confidence, you will be affected by residual fear. This fear will cloud your thinking. You again focus on the result, but now you are going to lose. The encouraging words of your family and friends are dreadful. You know your family and friends are not prophets. They do not really know that you will win. Also, they are not going to be in the ring with you. They are only providing you with words, and words are not going to do you any good. They do not see that you were matched with a tough opponent. Forget about winning. Your mental imagery is of defeat.

This is the same nonsense that is found with hubris, but on the opposite spectrum. I am susceptible to this negative thinking when I have not slept the night before. The imagined Attila the Hun from the night before is still present, and he strikes me with doubt. Your imagination and thoughts will be different in content, but the effect of fear will be the same. Fear prevents you from recognizing that your doubt is unreasonable. If you think your opponent is tough, then he and the matchmakers think you are tough too. You would not be matched up with him otherwise. Your family and friends are not here at your bout to see you lose. They have seen you train and respect your hard work. They are supporting you because they believe you will win.

The right amount of confidence will come to you when you stay focused on your preparation and give no mind to the result.

By focusing on what you have done, you provide a foundation for the appropriate amount of confidence.

The foundation for my confidence is the thought that now, right now, I am making it official. In the minutes before I go up those steps into the ring, I reflect on the work I have put in in preparation for the bout. Did I work out before I went to the office? Yes. Did I spar that fourth round when I was tired? Yes. I worked hard, and all there is to do is make this hard work official. The thought of "making it official" gives me the right amount of confidence. The is the same type of sentiment expressed by Muhammad Ali when he said, "The fight is won or lost far away from witnesses—behind the lines, in the gym, and out there on the road, long before I dance under those lights."

Unfortunately, making it official is a sentiment that has been unavailable to me at times. This occurs when I know deep down that I have not trained as hard as I should. Making it official is no longer a valid belief I can rely on. Confidence is still needed though. For these times, I rely on other thoughts. For example, I take thoughts into the ring that there is always a "puncher's chance" and boxers know "it just takes one." Obviously, it is better to be prepared than lucky, but luck may come my way. Believing that luck is with me is better than doubt. You have license to use whatever thoughts are available to make sure you walk up those steps into the ring with confidence.

The Opening Bell

Once in the ring, you will have a short meet and greet with your opponent as the referee motions you to the center of the ring. This is a civil courtesy, where the referee provides final instructions and makes sure you both have mouthpieces. You then return to your respective corners and wait momentarily until the opening bell. You might still have some anticipatory anxiety here, but once the opening bell sounds, it is officially gone. Physically, you step forward and meet your opponent to begin the physical combat. Mentally, you will box smart and fight the negativity of fear.

While we are all unique, there are some generalities every boxer experiences once he is face to face with his opponent. For instance, when I box well I have simple, positive thoughts. When I do not box well, I have diverse and complicated thoughts that are usually negative. There are many factors that can promote either mental state. In general terms, the better you have control of fear, the better you think and box.

Boxing Smart

The only way you box smart in the midst of a competitive bout is if you are calm. This serenity allows your brain and body to do the majority of the work during the bout. Being calm, you are allowing your brain and body to react to the situations as they present to you. When you are consciously thinking, you have simple concrete thoughts of what you need to do, such as "hit the body," "work," and "keep your chin down." If you do have thoughts about your opponent, they are observed vulnerabilities, such as "he's breathing hard, so go!" or "his hands are down." You tire as the bout progresses, but this fatigue is expected and not draining as the movements in the ring are flowing in your favor. The boxing strategy you are employing now is working. Your success is comforting and eliminates the negativity of fear. You are in control of your fear. Mentally, between rounds, you listen to your seconds in your corner, note the strategic recommendations, and rise from the stool with the thought, "I've got this."

Boxing Stupid

I am an expert at boxing stupid. I share this expertise to shed light on mental states to avoid. In these instances, when I box stupid, I allow fear to control me. I am no longer calm. My brain is now too muddled with negativity to allow my body to react to the immediacy of the bout. My negative thoughts interfere with my instincts. I am slower and directionless.

The remedy is to calm down and return my focus on what I need to do. I am assisted in this by my seconds between rounds. Simple directions, such as to breathe, are helpful. Also, in the midst of the adrenaline rush that fear prompts, I can only absorb one or two instructions between rounds. Emphatic directions to breathe and calm down work for me. I can then regain some serenity. My brain is freed from distraction, so my body can box as I have prepared it to do.

Unfortunately, there are times when this respite does not come soon enough. My fear escalates. If I let the pressure of the bout get to me, which is succumbing to fear, I focus more on the negative. For example, thinking how much time is left in the round and how tired I am does not make the time pass quicker or make me less tired. These thoughts also prevent me from boxing smart. I focus on my fatigue instead of my boxing.

Through experience, I have learned to recognize these unproductive thoughts during a round. This is my SOS signal that I need to calm down, regain my composure, control my fear, and box smart. The signal is therapeutic in itself. Now boxing smart, I am less frustrated with fatigue. The fatigue is expected, and I am confident I will continue to box to the end of the round like I should.

This recognition and learned composure has taken some time. Before boxing could teach me this, fear would rise to a point where I was overwhelmed. Not having yet learned the lessons in composure required to box smart, I would get angry.

Anger is a crude emotion. In simple terms, anger is an immature demonstration to others that I am upset. I imagine anger served me well when I was a baby, but it was to my detriment in the ring. Anger showed my opponent and the judges that I was upset. Witnessing my anger, it was not difficult for them to conclude that I was upset because I was not boxing well. Showing anger in itself caused me to lose favor in the judges' eyes and emboldened my opponent. I was not awarded points for anger.

The smart boxer does not get angry, but every boxer is vulnerable to anger. I was most vulnerable to anger when I was getting punched in the face. Getting punched in the face is a given in boxing. All boxers, even the best defensive boxers, such as Floyd J. Mayweather, get punched in the face. I knew before I ever first stepped into the ring to expect punches to the face. However, I did not know how angry this would make me.

When first boxing, absorbing physical punishment and losing were my anticipated fears. As a novice, I did not know that punches to the face are an emotional assault as well as a physical one. I had no idea how embarrassing it is to be punched in the face on a raised stage where spectators have a clear view. Without any consideration given to the potential damage inflicted, it is humiliating. No one looks cool when getting punched in the face.

This emotional assault would take place when I was full of fear and had not yet learned to control it. The fear enhanced my perceived humiliation. I was very upset. I then turned to anger. I would see red, the anger coursing through my body and brain. This anger would take away my humiliation and fear, as well as my composure.

With anger, I would focus on my opponent with thoughts such as, "Goddamnit! He just punched me in the face. F*** YOU!" Fueled by anger, with a boost in strength and fury, I would start punching with unbridled aggression. However, there were no smarts behind this angry attack. My heavy-handed punches would miss, disrupting my balance and movement. Also, I soon learned that anger is transient. Once gone, I was left with exhaustion. The fear returned. In such a state, I was more susceptible to being punched in the face, which started this whole process in the first place.

Anger is the apex of boxing stupid. It is a normal reaction to try to punch someone back after being punched. However, when boxing smart, this urge needs to be suppressed as your guard is down every time a punch is thrown. From your opponent's viewpoint, every punch you throw leaves an opening to hit you. When getting punched in the face, the correct response is to make adjustments. With experience, you learn the restraint to do this. You also learn, with time, the incorrect response is to get angry.

The Final Bell

The final bell at the end of the bout is a relief. Physically, boxing is draining. You will be tired. Mentally, the anticipatory anxiety and fear you have been experiencing for quite some time now is gone. You and your opponent celebrate this relief by touching gloves or by an embrace. Hugging someone after he has been trying to knock your head off is another one of the paradoxes in boxing, but it comes naturally. It is an acknowledgment of the physical and mental effort that you both have expended in the ring, and a mutual understanding that this effort brought out the best in both of you.

AMATEUR BOXING: MENTAL STRESS & STRENGTH

As you walk toward your corner to have your headgear and gloves removed, you have a premonition as to whether you won, lost, or if the bout was close. Soon, you are motioned by the referee to the center of the ring, where the referee will clasp each of your wrists. When the winner is announced, his hand will be raised by the referee. As is custom and a demonstration of sportsmanship, each boxer will then congratulate each other.

Having your hand raised as the winner is a great feeling—you did it. Conversely, it is a disappointment to lose. Much time and effort has been expended in the preparation for these three rounds of the bout, and such a denouement does not seem fair. This is why a referee will sometimes raise the hands of both boxers after the winner's hand has been raised and they have congratulated each other. It is recognition of the significance of the efforts of both boxers.

Winning or losing also typically comes with some token recognition in the form of a belt, trophy, medal, ribbon, etc. The token depends on the caliber of the amateur boxing show or tournament. In the end, the feelings associated with a win or loss are fleeting, lasting from hours to days. Soon you will be back in your regular day-to-day life. The mental stress of boxing is behind you.

Life without this stress is fine with no anticipatory anxiety or fear to derail the joys that abound. You settle back into your regular place in the world, doing the things that you do. This is fine. Your life is yours and you make the most of it. You enjoy what you do, what you have, and especially that you can share all of this with loving family and friends. Life is good.

No matter if life is good, the experience of amateur boxing attunes you to an inner quality that you may not have known you had. This quality is difficult to define, but a part of you now better appreciates life in full, a fuller understanding of what being alive really is. Once awoken, this quality is hard to suppress, and in boxing is referred to as the "itch."

The itch cannot be excised or placated. It is part of you now. It was always part of you. It arrives upon delivery. It is inherent in all of us. Amateur boxing just brings out this itch. Once you have stepped out of the ring, some time down the line, whether life is good or bad, you will walk back into the gym, wrap your hands with a smile, and get ready to do it all again.

Part III
WHY BOX?

WHY BOX WHEN THERE is so much stress involved? To get the itch seems like a silly answer, especially when the sport, in essence, is a fist fight. At first blush, it is easy to discount boxing. The argument against boxing can be summarized simply by saying that boxing is violent. One could argue that boxing is legalized assault and battery with a potent weapon—one's fist. As such, permanent injury and death are, not surprisingly, a result. As for amateur boxing, training people to inflict such harm, whether intentional or not, is criminally complicit. Those seconds and spectators exhorting the boxers are accessories to the crime. Furthermore, boxing is a remnant of our barbaric past. Civilization long retired fist fighting as an acceptable expression of distress and as a solution for dispute. If it is even considered innate to the human condition, it is vestigial. Like the inflamed appendix, boxing should be excised before inflicting further damage.

This argument against boxing, including amateur boxing, is reasonable and, based on the policy statements recommending a ban on amateur boxing, has some weight among physicians. However, the seasoned clinician recognizes that violence is ubiquitous (war, neglected neighborhoods, effects of alcohol and drugs combined with weapons, etc.), and boxing is no more violent than life itself. This is especially true as it relates to amateur boxing. To focus on and chastise amateur boxing is an attempt to treat nonexistent pathology. While the violence in the ring is real, the danger is mitigated by reasonable and enforced safeguards.

Maybe the safeguards provided in amateur boxing are not enough for some, and the violence of the sport is of such prominence that it overrides any potential benefits. I understand this. However, when properly examined, amateur boxing does have many benefits that make it worthwhile. First and foremost, amateur boxing does not promote violence outside the ring.

From a physical standpoint, amateur boxing is not a catalyst for violence. In other words, the violence in the ring does not prime the boxer to be violent when stepping out of the ring. After a bout, the exhausted boxer does not want to "play two," as enthusiastically endorsed by Chicago Cub Ernie Banks (1931–2015). One bout is enough for the day. One does not have the strength to go out looking for another fight. Also, the mental restraint that comes with boxing smart mitigates provocation and promotion of violence outside the ring. Boxers are trained to be calm in the face of violence. The boxer who boxes smart has developed an appreciation for its effectiveness. Brains trumps brawn, and this is an intelligence that may be more powerful than the education obtained from book learning. Amateur boxing requires and fosters this intelligence and restraint. This, in itself, is an antidote to violence outside the ring.

While most people do not enter a boxing gym to learn to be less violent, they will develop the strength to be so. That amateur boxing can be used to curb violence is not odd for those who know the sport. For example, the Police Athletic League (PAL) was formed in the early twentieth century to give wayward youth a productive activity to stay out of trouble. Amateur boxing was one of its original activities and continues to this day.

Amateur boxing offers much more than being a remedy for youthful problems. People are prompted to walk into a boxing gym or bring their children to learn how to box for many reasons. Common reasons are a new way to get into physical shape, to develop some skills to defend oneself, and the challenge itself. Boxing training is rigorous and efficient. Physical improvements support the decision to engage the sport.

What becomes more apparent with time are the mental benefits. Boxing provides as much mental vigor as physical. The usefulness of amateur boxing is, arguably, based more so on mental benefits than physical ones.

Eight
MENTAL BENEFITS

WHETHER YOU BOX TO get in shape or to compete, one of the appealing mental benefits is that boxing is not boring, which makes it fun. There are so many different boxing skills and strategy to learn that your brain will be continually engaged. Even when practicing a skill repeatedly, this is not mundane, as you need to consistently focus on doing it correctly. Also, if you have never punched anything, the boxing gym is the time and place to do it. Using your fists as they are designed to be used is, simply, fun. It is similar to the experience of driving a sports car as fast as it should be driven, but much safer.

That boxing is fun makes it easier to complete the physical workouts. A further reward for your efforts is that you will soon see physical improvements. Being in good physical condition and the resulting aesthetics will make anyone feel better about themselves. Also, regular exercise triggers the release of endogenous opioids in the brain, such as beta-endorphin. These naturally occurring opioids cause an elevation in mood. This event is popularly referred to as an "endorphin rush." Why exercise causes this release is unknown. It may provide reinforcement for regular exercise by elation, as well as decreasing perceptions of fatigue and pain. Whatever the case, physical activity on a regular basis evokes positive emotions and lowers the emotional stress that accumulates normally on a day-to-day basis

Inner Pride

The positivity associated with boxing makes the discipline required to improve a bit easier. Also, the improvements in boxing that come with practice provide a sense of satisfaction and accomplishment. Your initial ill-coordinated movements become more graceful with experience, and pride emerges.

This well-deserved pride is primarily internally generated. Developing an inner pride is important in boxing. This is what you need to rely on to assess your progress as you get ready for competition. Boxing, unlike some martial arts and many other sports, does not mark progress with completion of stages. Other than the number of bouts and records in these bouts, which is only obtained through competition, there are no set criteria to mark your progress in training. There are no external markers such as color of belts, times, or grades. With this lack of external markers of progress, you must rely on yourself. Your pride in your boxing proficiency and progress is based on an honest assessment of yourself.

With boxing, as seen with most endeavors, you soon learn that hard work is needed to improve. Hard work is the basis for your pride. It is what marks your progress. Moreover, you put the hard work to box better because this is what works. This hard work requires effort and self-discipline. This aspect of boxing

MENTAL BENEFITS

strengthens your character. Hard work is not only what you do, but also who you are.

Respect, Humility, and Empathy

Boxing is hard work, and no one beside you is going to do the hard work needed to improve. This inner pride, a well-deserved result of the hard work you have expended, will empower you with a new sense of self-respect. You now have been doing something you may not have thought you could have done, and you respect yourself for this. However, you also develop an appreciation that your progress has not been a solitary endeavor. Boxing is not a team sport, but you need a team behind you. You have required instructors, who are your coaches, trainers, and fellow boxers. People with more skill and experience than you are taking the time to share their knowledge to make you better. Respect for instructors, your team, is the natural progression of this process.

However, your team can only do so much to further your progress. You cannot learn defensive boxing, or, for that matter, effective offense by drill or bag work. A bag never punches back. You need to spar. And, in order to improve, you need to spar boxers better than you. In boxing, it is understood that in order to learn to avoid being punched, you will have to be punched. This is a humbling experience. You will be punched. You will get tired. You will be humbled.

Humility may seem like the antithesis of pride and a less desirable trait for the boxer. It is not. Humility is a counterweight to pride, and this is a positive action. Humility provides a benchmark for improvement. The boxing ring is an honest place. Having a sincere appreciation of where you are and where you can go is a requirement for improvement. You aspire to be the golden boxer, not the gilded one. A bit of humility will help you get there.

Humility also goes hand in hand with empathy. In part, this is due to apprenticeship, the same process of education that is the core of a medical education. In medicine, the first couple of years of medical school consists of book learning, specifically, the vocabulary and basic information to solve medical problems. The remainder of training is applying this information under the guidance of more experienced physicians. The mantra of "see one, do one, teach one" is the foundation of a medical education. It has been this way since Hippocrates (460–370 BC). Boxing follows this same apprenticeship model. Learning the different punches, footwork, and defense is the new vocabulary for the boxer. Applying this information in a skillful manner requires significant work coupled with teaching and guidance from an experienced boxer. Boxing is referred to as the "sweet science," as a nod to the development of this expertise.

In your study of the sweet science, when you first receive your lesson in humility, you will be humbled by a boxer who at one time was in your shoes. He will know firsthand of the frustration, embarrassment, and disappointment you are feeling. He will empathize with you, and typically express this by offering advice and encouragement as you spar. You will return the favor with a boxer who is less proficient. Empathy also emerges at the end of competition. After the violence has been dispensed, you will experience a sense of relief and satisfaction. This feeling is shared by your opponent. He just went through the same experience you did. The feeling of "I just did this" is coupled with the feeling that "we just did this." You have now made a friend. After the thrill of winning or disappointment of losing has passed, both boxers can meet and still feel that sense of satisfaction of doing something very hard, together.

Resilience

If you have boxed in an amateur bout, then you are a boxer. All amateur boxers know that each bout has a winner and a loser. Losing is fact. And losing is not fun. You have spent much time and effort in preparation for the three rounds. The disappointment of a loss is a tough emotional landscape to navigate. To get your mental bearings righted, you have to understand that, while you lost, you are not defeated.

Amateur boxing encourages this understanding. A seasoned boxer is not defeated by a loss. Losses are expected. The loss is only a result, a result that does not change no matter how much he dwells on it. Instead, his performance is what he dwells on and gains from. The bout has provided him a forum for an honest appraisal. He has learned that every loss is an opportunity to critically review what he can do better. His coaches and fellow boxers have provided constructive criticism. With the support from those in the gym, he has also looked inward and critiqued himself. He has received the correct information to box smarter, and he applies this knowledge in the gym. He is soon back in the ring, boxing smarter.

Losing is commonplace in amateur boxing. It has to be. Losing is valued curriculum in a boxing education. You gain from it. You move forward. You feel better with this merit-based progress. You should. The disappointment of the loss is gone, replaced with justified optimism. Your day will come. Until that day arrives, you continue to put the time and work in to box smarter for your next bout. This is a demonstration of resilience, and is inherent to the sport. With amateur boxing, you become resilient. This is who boxers are.

Even though amateur boxing has much mental stress, it also has mental benefits that are not readily apparent from outside the ring. (see Table 8.1)

Table 8.1: Mental Benefits of Boxing

▪ Empathy	▪ Intelligence	▪ Respect
▪ Humility	▪ Mood Elevation	▪ Restraint
▪ Inner Pride	▪ Resilience	▪ Stress Release

This is an admirable list that will enhance your emotional development. These characteristics make you a person who is more comfortable with himself and has more meaningful relationships with others. Amateur boxing helps you become the person you want to be.

These are not the only reasons why you box. You are born with an ingrained ability to fight, not for your wants, but for your needs. You box for the mental strength needed outside the ring.

Nine
OUTSIDE THE RING

Outside the ring, the boundaries are blurred. What corner is your corner may not be easily identified. Your seconds may not be there at the end of the round. Also, the rules are not clear. You find out during these fights that the rules have changed, and the officials neglected to inform you. These fights are more chaotic and confusing than in the ring. The punches come from improbable angles and with such speed that you cannot see them coming. In these fights, you may be punched in the face before the opening bell has rung. Outside the ring, in the real world, the fights are not fair.

You do not ask for these fights. No one does. Life makes these arrangements without your consent. Life matches you with sudden death or serious illness of a loved one, divorce, a failed business, etc. These are dangerous opponents. They can damage you. Understandably, no matter your specific opponent, all of these fights evoke mental stress. This mental stress is the same, but more pronounced than what you have experienced in amateur boxing.

You may be overwhelmed by mental stress in these fights. This mental stress is too intense and persistent to be used to your advantage. Instead of mobilizing you with heightened awareness, mental stress paralyzes your thoughts. Your thinking is slow. You no longer respond quickly or accurately. You are drained.

In this compromised state, these fights may bring out the worst of you. You become angry and are without restraint. You then look inward for relief, but find only pity and despair. You need respite, but the fight continues.

All is not lost. You have what you now need. You have called on it before, and you call on it now. At this time, during these fights, you call out for courage.

Courage

> "Courage is allowed to be chiefly natural, and probably owing, in a great measure, to the complexion and constitution of our bodies, and flowing in the different texture of the blood and juices; but, surely, it may be admitted, that it is not only acquired, but strengthened, by use and familiarity with danger."
>
> — Pierce Egan *Boxiana*, 1830

Pierce Egan (1772–1849) was a proud British writer who devoted a good portion of his professional work to boxing. Not only did he write of the contests between the boxers, but also wrote of boxing history, diet, strategy, and the training needed to be successful. Also, as addressed in the quotation above, he wrote of courage and offered the display and development of courage as evidence to dispel the "sneers of the fastidious and cant of the hyper-critics" who might disapprove of boxing. Egan's writing is as entertaining now as it probably was to readers then.

Egan's description of courage is a punch that hits the mark. Courage is natural. We all have access to it, and it works inside us. Where it is in us defies any medical or scientific explanation. His attribution to flowing in our blood and juices cannot be discounted. There are no anatomical or physiological pathways of courage, no neuroimaging studies identifying areas of the courage circuit, and no medical tests to measure or determine if you have or lack courage. You will not find a definition of courage in a medical textbook. So, what is courage and where is it?

Courage is the mental strength to make a decision in the presence of fear. This mental stress is fear more so than anticipatory anxiety. Courage is needed more when danger is upon you. Courage is mental strength because it allows you to make a decision not dictated by fear alone. The subsequent decision and action are immaterial. You may be in a tragedy that is hopeless and loss is imminent. There is no decision that will allow you to win, but this does not mean you are defeated by fear and tragedy. You will not be defined by this tragedy, because you have the courage to find serenity in the throes of fear. You have found peace on your terms, and you now act with a calmness because you have summoned the courage to do so.

Courage is mental strength, but it does not reside in the brain. If it did, I would show you where it is. Rather, courage's location cannot be pinpointed to a set place, as it is not only in us, but also all around us. Courage is ubiquitous. Being ubiquitous, courage escapes scientific quantification and words seem inadequate. Perhaps courage is similar in substance to the glow of a lover or the glint in the eye of the mischievous. These are substances that are seen, felt, and move us without a clear material or scientific presence other than they are there. For example, I see and feel courage when my children try something new. I am provided courage when they share the joys and sorrows of their own lives. I am without fear at these times, and my serenity is a testament to the courage they have given me.

You do not need children to locate courage. Courage is everywhere and can be found in unusual places. My cactus has courage in it. I know this because my cactus has been with me for quite some time. My cactus, now known as the cactus, was purchased for my second grade landscape project. I was assigned to build a landscape of the American Southwest in a shoe box and kept the cactus in my bedroom after the project was dismantled. I never really paid much attention to the cactus, as my mother provided whatever care it needed, but it became a permanent part of the bedroom I shared with my brother.

When we moved from Grand Island, New York to Wichita, Kansas for my father's work, the cactus came too. I was twelve at the time. Being twelve, I was not in charge of packing and did not bring it, but it ended up being packed in one of the moving boxes. When unpacked, my mother placed it in a new pot and put it in the window well of the basement bedroom I shared with my brother. Again, I did not pay the cactus much attention. I did not have much interest in it. In high school, I was preoccupied with other pursuits. Sneaking out of the house at night to go out, when I was told not to, was one of these pursuits. When I returned, my parents would not open the locked house. These times, I had to sleep in my bedroom window well next to the cactus. It was quite uncomfortable.

When I went off to college, I took the cactus with me. Now I was in charge of caring for the cactus, which meant it was abused and neglected. At various times, locations, and roommates, its home served as a spittoon and ashtray. It received water when I had the thought, which was rarely, but it was still living when I was finishing up college. By this time, the cactus was no longer mine alone. My roommates, past and present, claimed some kinship with the cactus, as it too had made it through college. The consensus was that this is one tough cactus. We brought the cactus to our college graduation.

I continue to have the cactus. It has persisted through my life travels. Following tradition, it was at my wedding. And it stayed with me at my divorce. It has been in the same pot for the past fifteen years and the same location for the past ten. It does not do much, except grow slowly. This, though, is what it does and is. The cactus endures.

I see the cactus now and again when I am in the yard. Its sight is always comforting, and not only for me. When one of my college roommates went to the Mayo Clinic for evaluation and treatment of a confusing disease, he reached out to me. While we were talking, he asked about the cactus, questioning if it was still alive. I texted him a picture to prove the cactus was alive. He was pleased, and probably reassured. While we did not talk about it, we both know the cactus is full of courage.

Courage being ubiquitous, in and around us, does not mean that it is readily accessible. While fear is required for the emergence of courage, it is not a guarantee that it will arrive. The initial fear may be too overwhelming to even consider or have the ability to summon courage. Also, when your courage has not yet arrived, being in the throes of fear may cause you to try to avoid fear itself. This is natural too, but fear does not go away on its own. Trying to escape fear, for example, by resorting to drink or denial only delays or prevents the courage needed to persevere. The facsimile of courage supplied by alcohol or drugs does not cure fear. These substances temporarily deaden fear, while the danger festers and probably grows. Fear will reemerge stronger, causing you to wonder where your courage is and even if you have any.

Acquiring Courage

Acquiring courage is both easy and hard. The hard part needs to be done first. You have to acknowledge what is evoking fear. This is difficult. No one readily faces a situation or problem when it is scaring them already. Also, fear may affect your brain so that the situation or problem appears worse than it actually is.

You now do what you have been taught. While this is your fight, you are not alone. You have a team behind you. Obtaining guidance and encouragement from family, friends, religious, spiritual, and/or mental health professionals is how you fight these fights. They provide you with the perspective and support you need to face and accept what is fearful.

The next part is easy. You call for courage, and it comes. Who, what, where, and how you call for courage is up to you. The method does not matter. You now have faced and accepted what is fearful. When you have done the hard work of honestly facing what is causing your fear, courage will soon come to you after you call for it.

By calling for courage, you open your brain to let courage in. Courage needs this invitation. Calling for courage is an exercise of your conscious brain that you are ready to make a decision. This decision will be a conscious one, and conscious thought only occurs in the brain.

What if you are so fearful, you are tongue-tied and unable to call for courage? No worries. Courage understands that fear is impairing. Courage has no need for formalities, and not much care or use for semantics. The thought of "enough," is enough of an invitation.

You know when courage has arrived when you have serenity. Your thoughts are clearer and purposeful. Now, you are again in charge. You are no longer ruled by fear. This new found mental strength allows you to now make that decision. This is a decision on your terms, one that acknowledges the fear, but is not coerced by it.

Your fight is different now. The negativity has lessened. You are not engulfed by fear, which gives you a clearer perspective. You face your opponent with this clarity. You can also see beyond the fight, where there is peace. You are fighting with courage.

Fighting with courage takes practice. American writer and amateur boxer Ernest Hemingway (1889–1961) defined courage as "grace under pressure." Grace implies a sophistication of action that is only acquired and strengthened with practice. Amateur boxing provides a forum for this practice.

Amateur boxing presents danger in the context of safety and sportsmanship. The bout is regulated, dignified, and fair. The mental stress evoked in such a forum is measured. While real, mental stress is titrated to fit within the confines of the sport. This mental stress is less foreboding and more manageable than outside the ring. Nonetheless, its presence is felt. How this mental stress is felt is different for each boxer. What is the same for each boxer is the requirement to make decisions under this pressure.

Also, similar to the problems in life that require courage, amateur boxing mimics these experiences. Your problem, your opponent, is right in front of you. Your opponent has every intention to punch you, on a stage, in front of people you care about. You may pretend to be without fear, but you will and should be fearful. The opening bell is about to ring. The confrontation cannot be delayed once the bells rings. Your opponent is not going to leave the ring and go away. Other than the respite both of you take to recover between rounds, you cannot take a break. In the ring, you have to confront your opponent in the here and now and remain in that moment to succeed. This takes courage.

At the end of the bout, maybe your hand will be raised and you will have a win tallied in your record book. Congratulations. However, maybe your hand will not be raised. You thought you were going to win, but it was not your night. You have been beaten.

But you are not defeated, and every spectator is a witness to this. When you were walking up those steps to the ring, your ascent gave you a clear look at the audience as well as your opponent. Maybe there was some hesitation, but everyone saw you step through those ropes into the ring. You did it. While you may not feel courageous, you showed your courage by stepping into the ring. At this moment, we were all witness to the courage flowing in you. And we know that you just tallied a win in a larger ledger.

Without much argument, this is the most important reason why you box. You transverse through the mental stress of boxing to reach the apex of mental strength that is courage. This is also the most sound reason to support amateur boxing. One cheers the courage of the boxers for their display of it in the ring. Also, one cheers so courage may be summoned by them, outside of the ring, when it will be needed most.

Epilogue
RANDIE CARVER

I have been fortunate in my life. I have met and spent time with exceptional people, people who have influenced me not only by instruction, but also by their values. Through amateur boxing, I crossed paths with Randie Carver, one of these exceptional people.

I first met Randie at the Rosedale Boxing Club located at the Bell Recreation Center in Kansas City, Kansas in the summer of 1994. Conveniently, Bell Rec was across the street from the University of Kansas Medical Center. The Rosedale Boxing Club had one of the better amateur boxing programs in the city, and Randie was the top boxer of the club. While I was a few years older than Randie, his boxing ability and stature in the gym were intimidating. I shied away from introducing myself to him when I started going to the gym. One afternoon that summer, Randie made a beeline for me while I was doing some bag work. My first thought was "This is a good time for me to do something else. Randie probably needs to work with this bag." Before I could step away from the bag, Randie, with a wide smile, called out, "Hey, Nate," and extended his hand. My second thought was, "How does he know my name?"

Randie introduced himself not as the top boxer, but as someone who knew about phlebotomy and was told I was a medical student at KU. With a welcoming curiosity, Randie asked about my studies and apologized for not introducing himself sooner. We spoke for about five minutes, none of which was about boxing. Before Randie went back to his workout, he told me how glad he was that I was there at the gym, and if I needed any assistance to just ask him.

I was a bit surprised at this encounter as it was unexpected, but I felt pretty good inside. As I got to know Randie a bit more, making people feel good about themselves is what he did. Randie was positive. He was a guy you liked hanging around with.

Randie was also sincere and true to his word. Whenever I needed help, Randie would take the time to do so. When I was training to compete, he would jump in the ring for sparring sessions with me. Even though this made his day longer, Randie did it with a smile that was infectious and encouraging. I wanted to get better, in part, because Randie wanted me to. I also was motivated by witnessing the hard work he put in training. Randie's training was practically Sisyphean. In the heat and humidity of the Kansas summer, Randie would run up the hill adjacent to the gym, jog back down, and run right back up again. I tried to do this once with Randie. I lasted a short while until the hill beat me. Randie continued. He also invited me to come back the next day to do it again. I did not, but Randie did. Randie could beat the hill. Randie did so, over and over again.

Witnessing Randie's efforts and talents, it would be expected that he would box well. Randie did much better than well. He was a tremendous amateur boxer. Randie was one of the top-ranked

EPILOGUE: RANDIE CARVER

amateur boxers in the United States and won the 1995 National Golden Gloves title at 156 lbs. when I was at the gym. It was not surprising that Randie soon decided to become a professional boxer.

One of the traditions of professional boxing is the use of a moniker. I was at the gym when Randie was with a group discussing potential monikers. Being the smart guy that I am, I offered "The Kansas City Kid." This seemed like a good idea when it was in my head, but leaving my lips, my unsolicited suggestion was met by stares and silence. Randie eventually smiled, and with laughter replied, "Ahh, Nate, I'm no kid." Randie's laughter was contagious, which gave me enough time to get out of Dodge. I left the gym without harm.

However, I was soon back at the gym. I had an opportunity I could not pass up. I was entered in a weekend amateur boxing show in Nevada. Not Las Vegas, Nevada, but rather Nevada, Missouri. Nevada is a small town, about a hundred miles south of Kansas City. I was excited for this show. I had not much success boxing in the city, and I hoped the change in location would be good for me. The slower pace of the country was more my speed boxing as a medical student. The only problem was that Nevada was out in the country. The time and travel were inconvenient. I need not have worried about this because Randie offered to work my corner.

This was in the spring of 1996. Randie was starting on his professional career and had much more important priorities than being in my corner. Though, having Randie in Nevada was awesome. I was calm and confident. It almost seemed unfair, but I had taken my lumps in the city. I convinced myself that I deserved this retreat in the country.

In the ring, it sure did not feel as if I were in the country. My opponent was not taking it slow and easy. Even though Randie was in my corner, he was not in the ring with me. I lost. This was not part of my pre-bout script. The reality was harsh. I apologized to Randie when he was cutting off my hand wraps. Instead of acknowledging my apology, Randie just let me know he looked forward to seeing me at the gym on Monday.

On Monday, still feeling dejected and like a fraud, I walked up to the door at Bell Rec. I did not want to go in, but I owed Randie. If Randie showed up in Nevada, then I could show up at the gym. Walking into the gym, I was greeted with congratulatory handshakes. As always, Randie was already at the gym. Randie had shared the result from my bout before I arrived. I soon gathered from his account that I drew a "tough country boy." And I lasted the entire three rounds and did the Club proud by doing so. I felt much better leaving the gym than when I walked in. Randie was again doing what he always did—making the world brighter for those around him.

This was the beginning of the end of my medical school boxing chapter. Bell Rec closed in 1997 to accommodate the growing Medical Center, and I graduated medical school that spring to continue my training in California. During my internship and residency, when I was still practicing general medicine, I volunteered as a ringside physician for USA Boxing.

In the late summer of 1999, I was working at the Blue and Gold Tournament. This was a large, national amateur boxing tournament in Southern California, and my old coach from Kansas City, George Smith, was there. Randie was also at the tournament, but I had just missed seeing him. It had been almost three years since I had seen George, and he got me up to speed on Randie's career. Randie was undefeated, had won a National boxing title, and was in line to box for a professional World title. While I had

EPILOGUE: RANDIE CARVER

missed seeing Randie at the tournament, I would soon be able to see him on national television defending his title in Kansas City.

That September, I was so happy for Randie as I watched him step into the ring with the loud cheers of the Kansas City crowd. Then tragedy struck. Randie never stepped out of the ring and was pronounced dead some days later.

Almost twenty years have passed since Randie's death. Time has allowed some thought for reflection and understanding. As it turned out, Randie ended up with the perfect moniker, "The Natural." The Natural was perfect because it encompassed so much more than Randie's natural talent and dedication to boxing. Randie had many other natural talents and dedications. One of these was his life-affirming nature. But what made Randie special and rare is that he took the time and effort to share his positive way of living with those around him. Randie's natural generosity was uplifting and permanent. This was Randie's gift to all of us who knew him, a gift that lives beyond his life.

Considering how rare and valuable Randie was, the only way to make any sense of his death is through fate. The Fates spun a strong, vibrant thread that was Randie. This was a short thread, too short, but I was fortunate to be touched by his thread. Randie Carver was in my corner. Damn. What a joy.

BIBLIOGRAPHY

Agel J, Rockwood T, Klossner D. Collegiate ACL Injury Rates Across 15 Sports: National Collegiate Athletic Association Injury Surveillance System Data Update (2004–2005 Through 2012–2013). *Clinical Journal of Sports Medicine* 2016; 26(6): 518–523.

American Academy of Pediatrics, Council on Sports Medicine And Fitness; Canadian Paediatric Society, Healthy Active Living And Sports Medicine Committee. Policy statement—Boxing participation by children and adolescents. *Pediatrics* 2011; 128(3): 617–623.

Baird LC, Newman CB, Volk H, Svinth JR, Conklin J, Levy ML. Mortality resulting from head injury in professional boxing. *Neurosurgery* 2010; 67(5): 1444–1450.

Barr RG. Colic and crying syndromes in infants. *Pediatrics* 1998; 102 (5 Supple E): 1282–1286.

Bateson M, Brilot B, Nettle D. Anxiety: an evolutionary approach. *The Canadian Journal of Psychiatry* 2011; 56 (12): 707–715.

Bellinger B, St Clair Gibson A, Oelofse A, Oelofse R, Lambert M. Energy expenditure of a noncontact boxing training session compared with submaximal treadmill running. *Medicine & Science in Sports & Exercise* 1997; 29 (12): 1653–1656.

Bernick C, Banks S. What boxing tells us about repetitive head trauma and the brain. *Alzheimer's Research & Therapy* 2013; Jun 4; 5(3) 23.

Bianconi E, Piovesan A, Facchin F, Beraudi A, Casadei R, Frabetti F, Vitale L, Pelleri MC, Tassani S, Piva F, Perez-Amodio S, Strippoli P, Canaider S. An estimation of the number of cells in the human body. *Annals of Human Biology* 2013; 40(6): 463–471.

Boddy K. *Boxing: a cultural history.* Reaktion Books Ltd., London 2009.

Butler RJ, Forsythe WI, Beverly DW. A prospective controlled investigation of the cognitive effects of amateur boxing. *Journal of Neurology, Neurosurgery & Psychiatry* 1993; 56: 1055–1061.

Cannon WB. *Bodily Changes in Pain, Hunger, Fear and Rage: An Account of Recent Researches into the Function of Emotional Excitement.* D. Appleton and Company, New York 1915.

Chaabène H, Tabben M, Mkaouer B, Franchini E, Negra Y, Hammami M, Amara S, Bouguezzi-Chaabène R, Hachana Y. Amateur boxing: physical and physiological attributes. *Sports Medicine* 2015; 45(3): 337–352.

Egan P. *Boxiana; or, Sketches of Ancient and Modern Pugilism, from the Days of the Renowned Broughton and Slack, to the Championship of Cribb: Volume 1.* George Virtue, London 1830.

Ferreira MB, Garcia-Marques L, Sherman SJ, Sherman JW. Automatic and controlled components of judgment and decision making. *Journal of Personality and Social Psychology* 2006; 91(5): 97–813.

Fuster JM. *The Prefrontal Cortex.* 5th ed. Academic Press, New York 2015.

BIBLIOGRAPHY

Golkar A, Lonsdorf TB, Olsson A, Lindstrom KM, Berrebi J, Fransson P, Schalling M, Ingvar M, Öhman, A. (2012). Distinct Contributions of the Dorsolateral Prefrontal and Orbitofrontal Cortex during Emotion Regulation. *Public Library of Science One* 2012; 7(11): e48107.

Gray JA, McNaughton N. *The neuropsychology of anxiety: An enquiry into the functions of the septo-hippocampal system.* Oxford University Press, Oxford 2000.

Grupe DW, Nitschke JB. Uncertainty and anticipation in anxiety: an integrated neurobiological and psychological perspective. *Nature Reviews Neuroscience* 2013; 14 (7): 488–501.

Haglund Y, Eriksson E. Does amateur boxing lead to chronic brain damage? A review of some recent investigations. *The American Journal of Sports Medicine* 1993; 21: 97–109.

Harber VJ, Sutton JR. Endorphins and exercise. *Sports Medicine* 1984; 1(2): 154–171.

Horns J, Jung R, Carrier D. In vitrostrain in human metacarpal bones during striking: testing the pugilism hypothesis of hominin hand evolution. *Journal of Experimental Biology* 2015; 218: 3215–3221.

Jako P. Safety measures in amateur boxing. *British Journal of Sports Medicine* 2002; 36: 394–395.

Kandel ER, Schwartz JH, Jessell TM, Siegelbaum SA, Hudspeth AJ. *Principles of Neural Science.* 5th ed. McGraw-Hill, New York 2012.

Kenzie ES, Parks EL, Bigler ED, Lim MM, Chesnutt JC, Wakeland W. Concussion As a Multi-Scale Complex System: An Interdisciplinary Synthesis of Current Knowledge. *Frontiers in Neurology* 2017; 8: 513. doi:10.3389/fneur.2017.00513.

Kerr ZY, Pierpoint LA, Currie DW, Wasserman EB, Comstock RD. Epidemiologic comparisons of soccer-related injuries presenting to emergency departments and reported within high school and collegiate settings. *Injury Epidemiology* 2017; 4(19): doi:10.1186/s40621-017-0116-9.

Loosemore MP, Butler CF, Khadri, A, McDonagh D, Patel VA, Bailes JE. Use of Head Guards in AIBA Boxing Tournaments—A Cross-Sectional Observational Study. *Clinical Journal of Sport Medicine* 2017; 27(1): 86–88.

Loosemore MP, Knowles CH, Whyte GP. Amateur boxing and risk of chronic traumatic brain injury: systematic review of observational studies. *British Journal of Sports Medicine* 2008; 42(11): 564–567.

Martland HS. Punch drunk. *Journal of the American Medical Association* 1928; 91(15): 1103–1107.

McCrory P, Zazryn T, Cameron P. The evidence for chronic traumatic encephalopathy in boxing. *Sports Medicine* 2007; 37(6): 467–476.

McIntosh AS, Patton DA. Boxing headguard performance in punch machine tests. *British Journal of Sports Medicine* 2015; 49(17): 1108–1112.

McLatchie G, Brooks N, Gailbraith S. Clinical neurological examination, neuropsychology, electroencephalography, and computed tomographic head scanning in active amateur boxers. *Journal of Neurology, Neurosurgery & Psychiatry* 1987; 50: 96–99.

Ochsner KN, Silvers JA, Buhle JT. Functional imaging studies of emotion regulation: A synthetic review and evolving model of the cognitive control of emotion. *Annals of the New York Academy of Sciences* 2012; 1251: E1-24.

BIBLIOGRAPHY

Ohno S. The reason for as well as the consequence of the Cambrian explosion in animal evolution. *Journal of Molecular Evolution* 1997; 44 Suppl 1: S23-27.

O'Sullivan DM, Fife GP. Impact attenuation of protective boxing and taekwondo headgear. *European Journal of Sport Science* 2016; 16(8): 1219–1225.

Pires-daSilva A, Sommer RJ. The evolution of signaling pathways in animal development. *Nature Reviews Genetics* 2003; 4(1): 39–49.

Roberts AH. *Brain damage in boxers: a study of prevalence of traumatic encephalopathy among ex-professional boxers.* Pitman Medical Scientific Publishing Co., London 1969.

Rosen JB, Schulkin J. From normal fear to pathological anxiety. *Psychological Review* 1998; 105(2): 325–350.

Ross RT, Ochsner MG Jr. Acute intracranial boxing-related injuries in U.S. Marine Corps recruits: report of two cases. *Military medicine* 1999; 164(1): 68–70.

Sarna SK. *Colonic Motility: From Bench Side to Bedside.* Morgan & Claypool Life Sciences, San Rafael, CA 2010. Available from: https://www.ncbi.nlm.nih.gov/books/NBK53477/

Sethi NK. In Response to: Use of Head Guards in AIBA Boxing Tournaments—A Cross-Sectional Observational Study. *Clinical Journal of Sport Medicine* 2018; 28(1): e1.

Steimer T. The biology of fear- and anxiety-related behaviors. *Dialogues in Clinical Neuroscience* 2002; 4(3): 231–249.

Stewart WF, Gordon B, Selnes O. Prospective study of central nervous system function in amateur boxers in the United States. *American Journal of Epidemiology* 1994; 139: 573–599.

Stiller JW, Weinberger DR. Boxing and chronic brain damage. *Psychiatric Clinics of North America* 1985; Jun; 8(2): 339–356.

Tallinen T, Chung JY, Rousseau F, Girard N, Lefèvre J, Mahadevan L. On the growth and form of cortical convolutions. *Nature Physics* 2016; 12: 588–593.

Yoshimura S, Okamoto Y, Yoshino A, Kobayakawa M, Machino A, Yamawaki S. Neural Basis of Anticipatory Anxiety Reappraisals. *Public Library of Science One* 2014; 9(7): e102836.

Zazryn T & McCrory P. *Boxing, in Epidemiology of Injury in Olympic Sports, Volume XVI* (eds Caine DJ, Harmer PA & Schiff MA), Wiley-Blackwell, Oxford, UK. 2009. doi: 10.1002/9781444316872 .ch7

Zhang Z, Lei Y, Li H. Approaching the Distinction between Intuition and Insight. *Frontiers in Psychology* 2016; 7, 1195: http://doi.org/10.3389/fpsyg.2016.01195

About the Author

NATHAN E. LAVID, MD, is a clinical and forensic psychiatrist. He received his medical degree from the University of Kansas School of Medicine. He interned and completed his psychiatry residency in the Departments of Medicine, Neurology, Pediatrics, and Psychiatry and Human Behavior at the University of California, Irvine. He then completed a fellowship in forensic psychiatry at the Institute of Psychiatry, Law & Behavioral Sciences at the University of Southern California, where he was on Faculty as Clinical Instructor at the Keck School of Medicine of USC. He is licensed to practice medicine in the states of California and New York, Diplomate of the American Board of Psychiatry and Neurology, Distinguished Fellow of the American Psychiatric Association, and Psychiatric Expert for the Medical Board of California. He worked on Diagnostic and Statistical Manual of Mental Disorders (DSM-5) as a Field Trials Collaborating Physician Investigator. A former Review Editor for *Frontiers in Forensic Psychiatry*, he has published one other book, and multiple book chapters and professional articles in psychiatry. He lives in Long Beach, California.

www.ingramcontent.com/pod-product-compliance
Lightning Source LLC
Chambersburg PA
CBHW030327080526
44584CB00012B/738